Computerized Work Management Systems for Utility and Plant Operations

Computerized Work Management Systems for Utility and Plant Operations

Roopchan Lutchman

DES*tech* Publications, Inc.

Computerized Work Management Systems for Utility and Plant Operations

DEStech Publications, Inc.
1148 Elizabeth Avenue #2
Lancaster, Pennsylvania 17601 U.S.A.

Printed in the United States of America
10 9 8 7 6 5 4 3 2 1

Entry under main title:
   Computerized Work Management Systems for Utility and Plant Operations

A DEStech Publications book
Bibliography: p.
Includes index p. 205

ISBN: 1-932078-30-4

Contents

Preface

PURPOSE OF THIS BOOK

The idea for *Computerized Work Management Systems for Utility and Plant Operations* was born out of the frustration I saw at many client sites. In all the industries I have worked in, I have come across companies who have struggled hopelessly to find and implement a computerized work management system (CWMS) that met the expectations of all concerned. There are many companies who do not have a system and are not sure how to get one. There are many companies who have a system, spent hundreds of thousands of dollars to acquire and implement the system and are very dissatisfied with it. And there are many companies who have a system and think that it is providing significant value to their operations, when in reality there is so much more they can get out of it.

The information provided in the book is practical and is based on my actual experiences with companies in the justification, selection, acquisition and implementation phases of a CWMS project. Additionally, I have considered the CWMS project an integral part of implementing best practices. In this approach, the CWMS is a computerized tool that a company can use to do work (any kind of work) in a cost-effective manner. This book serves to educate people on CWMS in general and its value to the business industry today. It is also intended to be a step by step guide to help people identify the need for a CWMS, justifying the purchase of one, selecting the right CWMS for your operations, achieving a successful implementation, make effective use and provide adequate support of the system.

Computerized Work Management Systems for Utility and Plant Operations is based on my actual experiences at client sites as a maintenance consultant. My experiences teaching the subject at Durham College in Ontario, Canada provided a further insight into the frustration people found when they tried to find a CWMS solution for their companies. I identified a number of problems that I addressed in various ways during these assignments. Also, at maintenance forums and workshops that I participated in, a number of these problems surfaced as major stumbling blocks to a successful CWMS. The following are some of the major problems and questions that I identified:

- How do we recognize that our company needs a CWMS?
- How do we justify a CWMS to senior management?
- How do we define what we want in a CWMS?
- The union and employees do not support our proposal to implement a CWMS.
- There are over 250 CWMS solutions varying in price from $2,000 to over $1 million. How do we select one from this listing?
- We have a CWMS implemented but it is not working for us. We use extra labor just to run the system.
- We have an old CWMS solution and would like to move to one of the more modern systems but are not sure how to do this.
- Our CWMS solution provider is no longer operational and we have no support or source code.
- Our CWMS implementation has been going on for the last two years and these consultants seem to live in our company.

In all the situations that these problems arose I was able to provide solutions to the client that worked to their satisfaction. Some of the solutions were pretty simple and can be found in some publications, however there was not one source that I could look up and address all these issues. This book spans the full spectrum of the typical CWMS projects. It provides excellent advice and guidance for companies that have never used a CWMS. Companies that have a CWMS and are happy with the system can find value in the book by being able to review their system and squeeze some extra value out of it. The book is extremely useful to companies that would like to move up to the latest CWMS technology that is available.

The information provided is very practical and would appeal to maintenance and operations management personnel as well as shop floor personnel who play a key role in the success of any CWMS. The information is structured so that personnel can easily identify where they are in the CWMS process and can thus use it as a reference to move forward. The examples used to discuss methodologies and solutions to problems are practical and they can easily relate to them. The graphics are simple and provide value in explaining concepts as well as making them easy to remember.

The book also looks at the overall picture and ensures that the CWMS solution fits in well with the overall technology plan for other computerized solutions. It provides excellent advice and guidance for people to review their operations and implement improved practices in the area of Program Driven Maintenance, Predictive Maintenance and Total Productive Maintenance. The information covered in this book can also be easily applied to the selection and implementation of other major technology business tools.

Finally, this book is very valuable to maintenance professionals from an academic standpoint. It would be an excellent reference text for technical schools and universities for the relevant maintenance engineering courses.

Acknowledgements

To the many people who have influenced my thoughts and ideas and have encouraged me to write this book so that others can benefit. I would also like to thank my wife and children for giving me the support I needed to make this book a reality. Special recognition goes to Frank Godin for reviewing the draft manuscript and to Kelly Meighan for designing the book cover.

CHAPTER 1

Introduction to Computerized Work Management Systems

WHAT IS A CWMS?

CWMS is the abbreviation for computerized work management systems. Generally a CWMS is a software program or combination of programs that is displayed to the users as a number of modules. CWMS are designed to computerize the work management process (in particular, maintenance-type work) and its associated support processes (e.g., inventory, purchasing and capital projects). These computer software programs are designed to assist in the planning, management and administrative procedures required for effective work management. The CWMS is a business tool that allows control over the linked work and material processes and at the same time provides a means for collection of valuable cost and work history data.

These processes include work initiation (work request), planning and scheduling work orders work execution and closeout. In addition, the inventory and purchasing processes provide the necessary materials and services that facilitate work. All these processes are related to each other through workflow that allows the electronic simulation of business procedures. The CWMS is similar to other business applications in that it consists of system programs that provide certain functionality. Data can be created, stored and retrieved for use by the programs. The data describes the equipment, parts, jobs, crafts and all other items involved in the work process and is stored in the database that can be a separate program. The program or software code retrieves stored data, provides the ability to enter new data, creates new data based on math operations and can create information in the form of printed reports or screen displays.

Users of a CWMS work at a computer terminal and use printers to produce work requests, work orders, inventory pick lists, purchase requisitions, purchase orders and necessary reports. The system can run on a stand-alone personal computer (microcomputer), a networked minicomputer system, a mainframe computer or a client server system. The stand-alone personal computer unit is one in which the CWMS program and data are stored on the unit and also used to carry out the work process. A networked minicomputer system is generally a group of terminals connected to a powerful minicomputer. The program and data reside on the minicomputer, the display and data entry are done on the terminals. A mainframe is a large central computer in which all programs and data reside. Displays, data entry and operations are carried out on individual terminals. (Note that a minicomputer is a small version of a mainframe; it has about the same operating characteristics but is considerably less powerful and less expensive.) A client server system is a network of personal computers (called clients or workstations) connected to powerful computers called servers. The clients can store data, programs and perform operations or can access data and programs from the servers. This is the most popular type of system used to operate CWMS today. All of the above systems permit placing terminals on the desks of personnel who need to create work-related records, retrieve stored records, review history and prepare reports needed daily in the work management process.

THE HISTORY OF THE CWMS

The original method of documenting maintenance work on equipment was through the use of card files and is the precursor to the modern-day CWMS. The need to store great volumes of data for easy retrieval and manipulation into useful information led to electronic storage. With the advent of the information age, programmers developed software running on computers that filled this need. Two and one-half decades ago, CWMS were typically programs written for mainframe computers to manage the maintenance process and were referred to as Computerized Maintenance Management Systems (CMMS). They offered very basic features such as equipment configuration and history, work request, work order and the preventive maintenance process. Over the years, the CMMS evolved into complex integrated programs operating on minicomputers with a major focus on maintenance of equipment. The terminals were the typical green-colored ones and data entry or functions were strictly keyboard driven. These were functionally very rich, but did not provide the Windows look and feel of other client server business appli-

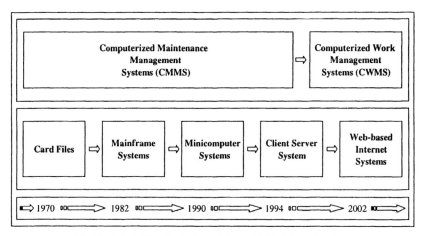

FIGURE 1.1 *The Evolution of the CWMS with Technology.*

cations. Pressured to provide the user friendliness and ease of use of other applications, a number of vendors developed Graphical User Interfaces (GUI) that simulated a Windows look and feel but did not provide the true power and flexibility of the client server system. Parallel to this development there was a shift in thinking to using software to manage all work instead of maintenance work and the term CWMS was born. Over the last five years, there was a distinct trend to have a CWMS running on desktop computers (client server systems) operating in the popular Microsoft Windows environment. The advances in object oriented (OO) technology have radically shaped and changed the CWMS in the Windows environment. Current research and development suggests that the CWMS is headed for mainstream Internet integration in the future. In addition, the use of the CWMS is now being expanded to include asset management-related business functions and some vendors are labeling their CWMS software as enterprise asset management systems (EAMS). A graphic depiction of the evolution of CWMS with technology is shown in Figure 1.1.

THE CWMS MARKET TODAY

Over the past years, senior management personnel paid to a lot of lip service to CWMS. Many companies invested in a CWMS but failed to gain any significant benefits from the system due to poor product choice, implementation or lack of support from staff and employees. As a result, the CWMS was generally relegated to a tool for the creation of sketchy work orders and for data collection. The result was a host of data that could not be trusted and, as such, was not relied upon. These companies found themselves in a vicious cycle of reactive maintenance and could not devote the necessary resources to implement and use the CWMS properly to get on the road to proactive maintenance.

As the squeeze came on to manufacture products or provide services more cost effectively, companies re-engineered themselves by making the production or the operations department very lean. They also introduced much more complex and automated equipment for which maintenance requirements were higher. The maintenance department was generally regarded as a necessary evil and this area was not generally targeted for re-engineering. Today, with the unrelenting pressure from competing industries, companies are slowly realizing that there is a wealth of savings to be made using a successfully implemented CWMS to execute a strategic approach to maintenance management and manage all work in a cost-effective manner. The CWMS also satisfies the need for proper documentation of work practices associated with ISO 9000 certification.

As a result, there has been a boom in the CWMS industry with a number of companies (>250) selling hundreds of CWMS products and re-

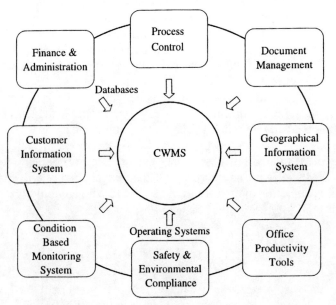

FIGURE 1.2 The CWMS in an Overall Technology Solution.

lated services. This boom is projected to continue well into the twenty-first century. The industry is projected to be in the area of $2 billion (US) and is a clear indication of the serious attention given to this business tool by senior management in industries today. One caution to the reader: a CWMS by itself is not the solution to business problems. Selecting the right CWMS in a market where packages may vary in price from $2000 to $1 million for a system can be quite a daunting task. The package selected must fit into an overall program to improve operations, must be part of an integrated technology solution with other business applications and must be successfully implemented. Proper use of an integrated tool to conduct business practices and create and use information from stored data is critical to achieving any benefits from the CWMS. Figure 1.2 gives a graphic view of a typical integrated solution.

APPENDIX 1.1 GUIDELINES FOR SEARCHING FOR CWMS VENDORS

(1) Letting the CWMS vendor find you
   (a) CWMS vendors are continuously looking for business opportunities and actively pursue any advertisements by companies requesting information on CWMS software solutions.
   (b) CWMS vendors also make regular cold calls on potential clients in their focus areas. In this regard, you may get solicitations for meetings or product demonstrations. You should take advantage of these opportunities to learn more about the product and the vendor. One note of caution, however, is to be careful not to get swayed by the "bells and whistles" and enter into any agreements before following the selection process recommended in this book.
(2) CWMS vendor listings in magazines and journals
   (a) Many of the reputable CWMS vendors regularly advertise their CWMS solutions in magazines and journals targeting specific industries. This can be a good source of information on CWMS vendors.
   (b) Some magazines and journals also regularly survey the industry and publish a listing of vendors by various categories (product modules, operating system, scalability, number of installed sites).
(3) CWMS vendor listings on the Internet
   (a) CWMS vendors (like many other product and service vendors)

have websites advertising their company and products. A search under the following categories should lead to information on potential CWMS vendors.

- computerized work management systems (CWMS)
- work management systems (WMS)
- computerized maintenance management systems (CMMS)
- maintenance management systems (MMS)
- enterprise asset management systems (EAMS)
- asset management systems (AMS)
- enterprise resource planning systems (ERPs)

(b) Many vendors advertise their products on popular websites related to the industries they are interested in.

(c) Some companies actually provide an online service (for a fee) to help companies find potential software solutions and vendors to meet their needs. These companies continuously scan the software industry for changes and keep their online database updated.

(4) Management consultant databases

(a) Management consultants who help clients improve their business practices, select and implement appropriate enabling technologies have updated listings of the various software vendors available to the selection process.

(b) These consultants usually provide an added bonus of having relevant experience with the vendors as well as the CWMS solution being offered. They are able to provide a feel for good and poor performers.

(c) Companies should be careful, however, when using consultant advice in this area to guard against the consultant's bias towards a particular software vendor with whom they may have a working relationship.

CHAPTER 2

CWMS—An Integral Part of Work Management Strategy

AN INTRODUCTION TO BEST PRACTICES

The term best practices has been bandied about over the years as the cure for all business ailments. In fact, many people are turned off by the many best practices concepts offered as solutions to problems. In helping clients improve their business practices and become competitive, past experience has shown a deep desire by clients for practical solutions that the workforce can easily relate to. This approach to best practices considers work to be the reason for existence (*raison d'être*), with all other business elements in a support role. Clients who embrace best practices concepts need to take their business from *reactive work* through the phase of *proactive work* with a vision of achieving *optimized work*. While these states of the work environment are typical, it is important to note that some companies may be able to identify with certain elements of all three states but a clear dominance in one particular area. These phases in the quest for excellence are shown in Figure 2.1 and are discussed in detail below (see also Table 2.1.)

Reactive Work

In reactive work there is little or no planning and scheduling of work. The prevailing atmosphere is one of frustration (sometimes desperation) to try and repair assets or perform a work order task immediately because of loss of revenue or a safety concern. In this environment reactive work can be over 75% with only 25% of the total work being proactive. There is a high cost associated with work execution that includes high labor

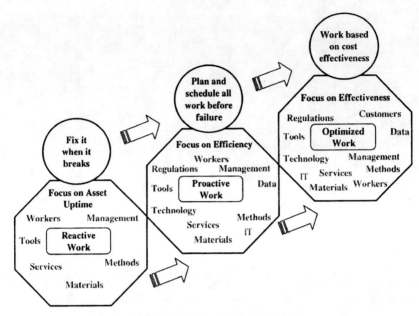

FIGURE 2.1 *Best Work Practices.*

(overtime), materials, services and opportunity due to equipment down-time. In addition, there can be high cost associated with secondary damage to equipment as a result of catastrophic failure. The following are brief descriptions of the roles of various resources in a typical reactive mode of performing work.

Workers

There is a deliberate organizational structure that supports silos of various groupings of personnel. This is particularly reflected in the maintenance and operations area. These workers do what they are told and talk to other departments by communicating to their supervisors who, in turn, speak to the supervisor of the other department. The message is then relayed to the workers in the other department through their supervisor. It is obvious that valuable time and resources are wasted in this type of an environment. Generally, workers know what has to be done to resolve an issue or a problem to complete a task or work order task properly and on schedule. However, the lack of empowerment to make decisions contributes significantly to the reactive way of working. Needless to say, the work force tends to lack commitment, dedication and motivation. It is in-

TABLE 2.1 Best Practices and Work Management Kinetics.

Work Resource	Reactive Work	Proactive Work	Optimized Work
Workers	Silos—operations, maintenance, not empowered, little multiskilling	Silos—operations, maintenance, however, better coordination between the groups	Work cells of empowered maintenance and operations personnel practicing total productive maintenance
Customers	Not focused on the customer	Very customer focused, every effort made to satisfy customers at a premium cost	Customer focused but based on cost effective quality of product or service
Asset	Poor reliability	Improved reliability at a premium cost	Cost effective reliability based on the needs of the user and regulations
Regulations	Unable to meet or struggle to meet requirements	Generally meet and exceed requirements	Consistently meet the necessary requirements
Management	Top down	Top down approach still prevalent, but better informal communication	Bottom up evidenced by great team dynamics, empowered workers with initiative and enthusiasm
Technology	Little or none	Stand-alone systems, generally dictated by corporate IT strategy	Best of breed business applications with flexible interfaces
Methods	Do what was done in the past, no documentation of procedures	Procedures and maintenance practices documented in a CWMS based on experience of users, PMs are time based. Good planning and scheduling	Procedures and maintenance practices documented in a CWMS-based RCM, PM is are quality based on appropriate predictive, condition-based monitoring techniques. Planning and scheduling involve maintenance and operation.

9

TABLE 2.1 (continued) Best Practices and Work Management.

Work Resource	Reactive Work	Proactive Work	Optimized Work
Services	Heavy dependence on outside services, no control	Good control of the use of services using a CWMS	Appropriate mix of services and internal work force for doing work
Materials	Poor availability, quality and stores service level, numerous satellite stores	Good inventory management, large centralized stores concept. Bill of materials associated with assets.	Good inventory management focused on optimal stores value, number of stock items and service level. Use of properly managed satellite stores and centralized stores. Appropriate mix of consignment and just-in-time inventory practices
Tools	Inadequate tools	Tools are made available for work order tasks, but little effort is made to procure tools to work smarter	Specialized tools associated with identifying potential failures and doing repairs before failure occurs. Appropriate tools for working smarter.
Data	Paper records, limited electronic data, questionable quality and integrity	Data is captured religiously throughout the work management process, however, the quality is suspect and little attempt is made to use the data for decision making	Data is routinely used to create much needed information for decision making, continuous improvement, improved asset reliability and drives the capital project program.

teresting to note in the reactive mode of working the operations staff think that their maintenance colleagues work very hard to keep assets operational. Maintenance staff sees themselves as firefighting heroes being called in to save the day on a regular basis. Recognition (and rewards) is based on how well they put out "fires."

Customers

In a reactive mode of operations, workers are too busy fighting fires, in a panic to get production back on track, that they rarely have the time to consider the end result of doing work. That is, satisfaction of the customer through a quality product, timely delivery and quality service. Customers' complaints as well as suggestions and promises to correct previous problems and foul-ups are lost in the daily frenzy to keep things ticking along.

Assets

In a reactive-type operation, assets are unreliable and the prevailing maintenance philosophy is "fix it when it breaks." There is usually a lot of obsolete equipment being maintained, lack of appropriate spares, and poor service from the stores and purchasing support group. Little effort is made to standardize equipment, parts and equipment performance levels.

Regulations

Reactive-type operations are characterized by numerous violations of safety, environmental and quality-type regulations. In many cases there are catastrophic failures, accidents and high costs associated with loss of assets, production opportunities and life. There are also many near-miss incidents that tend to go unnoticed or unrecorded.

Management

A top down management structure prevails in a reactive work environment. Everyone waits for directives, guidance and pronouncements from their immediate supervisors before acting. People can be disciplined for violating the reporting lines. Management decides on solutions to problems without the involvement of the workers. These solutions are then force-fed to employees without their being educated on the potential benefits. Workers feel that their views are not wanted or appreciated.

Technology

Technology is usually decided on by people (usually the IT department) who have no idea what the workers need in order to do their work order tasks and never thought about involving them in the selection and implementation process. Usually, technology solutions are simple stand-alone systems that were not selected with the overall technology solution in mind. Technology solutions that are selected are implemented and then people only use them if they are forced to. Workers tend to go back to the old ways of working at every opportunity that presents itself. These solutions place an additional workload on people who are already struggling with a reactive way of working. Training on the systems is limited and often very inadequate. Upgrades to new releases are major nightmares for workers and are usually implemented like the system itself—with little involvement of the end users.

Methods

Work practices are generally not standardized and are usually based on the experience of the individual. There is little or no documentation of practices. New employees depend heavily on experienced employees transferring knowledge during execution of the work order task and also on a personal cache of documents, files and manuals.

Materials

This type of operation is characterized by poor materials availability (both stores and non-stores), quality of materials and stores service level. In order to compensate for the inefficient stores service, numerous satellite stores (sometimes illegal) spring up throughout the operations. The result is clearly unacceptable.

Services

There is heavy dependence on outside services in order to satisfy the major demands on maintenance. There are generally problems associated with cost control and the quality of work order tasks done by outside contractors. In a union environment, existing agreements may limit the amount of service work done by outside personnel. Conflicts with the union on the issue of use of these services are not uncommon. Where the use of services is limited, the work is usually done through high overtime for maintenance employees.

Tools

There are inadequate tools to support the work execution process. Occasionally, people may purchase highly specialized tools (e.g., laser alignment units) but these are not used effectively and they sometimes end up in the tool room collecting dust.

Data

Data is typically represented by paper records and very limited electronic data of questionable quality and integrity. In most cases, work is initiated verbally, executed without any closeout information and any data stored as history. Many people responsible for maintenance functions keep personal records of work done and the data on assets to ensure that they can perform their work order tasks effectively. This information is usually limited to a select few personnel.

Proactive Work

In the proactive work phase there is control on the workload through effective execution of the work management process. This process is fully supported by other processes such as inventory, purchasing and accounts payables. There is good planning and scheduling with detailed work plans and all supporting resources available for work execution. It is not uncommon to find the percentage of planned work being close to 100% of all the work being done in this type of operation. There is, however, little focus on cost effectiveness and equipment reliability is sometimes achieved at a high cost (materials, labor, services and the opportunity cost associated with equipment downtime during repairs or overhaul). The following are brief descriptions of the roles of various resources and components in a typical proactive mode of performing work.

Workers

Silos are still very much evident, especially in the operations and maintenance areas. However, there is much better coordination between the groups as evidenced by an improved preventive maintenance program and better planning and scheduling. Operators and maintainers informally discuss problems and issues with a goal of being in control of the operations. The organizational structure still encourages a top down approach to communications and there is the tendency to lay blame when there is a problem rather that seek solutions.

Customers

There is an increased awareness that the real purpose of doing work is in some way related to customer satisfaction. Product quality or service level is considered as a performance indicator in addition to typical maintenance and operations indices such as equipment uptime and process rate. However, the effort to satisfy the customer is achieved at a premium cost because quality standards are regularly surpassed.

Assets

There is improved reliability through extensive planning and scheduling of work and a tendency to set up preventive maintenance work order tasks for all assets and components regardless of the criticality. As a result, equipment is usually shut down, serviced, overhauled or lubricated when there really is no indication of a problem. Reliability of equipment increases but at a premium cost. There is a high cost of labor, materials and services associated with the work management process. In addition, there is the opportunity cost associated with reduced process rate when equipment is out of service. This is sometimes overcome by using extensive overtime on the "off shift" hours to meet the preventative maintenance (PM) schedule.

Regulations

In a proactive work environment, regulatory requirements are easily achieved through improved equipment reliability and fewer process upsets. The number of safety and environmental issues are reduced, because there is better planning and scheduling and better control of the work management process. However, there is a tendency to ignore cost and, in most cases, surpass regulatory requirement, especially in the area of inspections and effluent quality. Standard approaches may be too costly for some equipment and may not be fully developed for others.

Management

The organization structure still encourages a top down approach to communications and there is the tendency to lay blame when there is a problem rather that seek solutions. Operators and maintainers informally discuss problems and issues with a goal of being in control of the operations. Workers are still not empowered to make decisions that speed up the work process and reduce non-value-added work. Workers still feel that their views are not wanted or appreciated. There is a lack of focus on asset criticality and a short-term approach to the PM process.

Technology

Technology is still based on stand-alone systems that have been generally defined, selected and implemented by corporate IT. Any interfaces are "hard wired" to the financial system to support general ledger (GL), payroll and accounts payables. Usually the system works well in allowing plant personnel to conduct the work management process using the CWMS tool. There is major reluctance to upgrade to newer releases or to take advantage of patches and error corrections because of the work associated with upgrading the individual interfaces.

Services

There is usually good control of services when they are initiated in the planning and scheduling process and procured through the purchasing module of the CWMS. The use of services is, however, not based on a clear evaluation of the cost effectiveness of in-house versus contract services.

Methods

Procedures and maintenance practices are documented in the CWMS based on the experience of users. This is reflected in the design of the preventive maintenance program in which PM is time based and there is very little effort to optimize these intervals. There is usually good planning and scheduling of all work orders including PM-type work orders. There is a tendency, however, to plan and schedule all work order tasks and this can easily result in a high-cost maintenance operation.

Materials

There is usually good inventory management which is dictated by the need to control the inventory and ensure that materials are always available to support the work planning process. This is usually achieved through the large centralized stores concept. It is driven by the use of bill of materials (BOM) associated with assets and the need to stock all the key items based on reorder points (ROP) and reorder quantities (ROQ). The high quality of service is usually achieved at the expense of large numbers of stock items, high inventory value and a higher cost of managing the stores.

Tools

Tools are generally made available for work order tasks, but little effort is made to procure tools to work smarter. The old way of working is simulated effectively on the CWMS and tools are usually tracked through the use of a tool room(s) set up in the inventory system. There is typically good management of the tool room. This is sometimes viewed by employees as micromanagement and there is a lack of confidence in the employees.

Data

New records are created routinely throughout the work management process and sent into history. Closeout information is very limited, the quality is sometimes suspect and little attempt is made to use the data for decision making. Cost information is sometimes incomplete or inaccurate and people rely on the accounting reports from the financial system for decision making related to cost.

Optimized Work

In an optimized work environment there is an appropriate mix of proactive and reactive work based on cost effectiveness. The optimum split is 75% proactive work and 25% reactive work in general. This split can vary by +/− 5 to 10% based on the type of industry.) This is achieved through the identification of critical equipment, selection of the appropriate repair tactics using reliability centered maintenance, prediction of potential failures using predictive maintenance and condition-monitoring techniques and the use of data for decision making. The underlying culture is one of continuous improvement and this is achieved through a team-based empowered organization working under total productive maintenance concepts. The following are brief descriptions of the roles of various resources in a typical optimized mode of performing work.

Workers

There are work cells of empowered maintenance and operations personnel practicing total productive maintenance. Operations personnel practice cleaning, lubrication, adjustments, inspections and do minor repairs (CLAIR). Maintenance personnel are freed up to do more core maintenance work such as major repairs, overhauls and predictive maintenance. There is good cooperation between operations and maintenance and everyone focuses on agreed-to performance targets. Maintenance trades are trained up in low level operations tasks for taking equipment out of service and recommissioning them without operator help.

Customers

Optimized maintenance is customer focused in an effort to produce a product or service of high quality. However, quality standards are closely monitored and kept within close limits in order to be cost effective.

Assets

Reliability centered maintenance (RCM) and predictive maintenance (PdM) are used in conjunction with preventive maintenance to do appropriate work on assets with a goal of extending the mean time between failure (MTBF) or reliability of assets. Data collected in the course of doing work using the CWMS are routinely used to evaluate and modify the work planned for assets. Cost effective reliability is usually achieved to satisfy the needs of the user, safety and environmental regulations.

Regulations

All work management efforts are done with the objective of consistently meeting the necessary requirements in addition to other operations and maintenance objectives. However, there is a deliberate attempt to be cost effective and not surpass these regulatory requirements.

Management

There is a bottom up approach to management that is evidenced by fewer levels of supervisory personnel in a team-based organization. Workers are empowered to think, they are provided with dependable data and performance measures and are given the responsibility to make decisions. The result is great team dynamics and empowered workers with initiative and enthusiasm who deliver high work quality and productivity. Workers feel that their suggestions and views are valued and appreciated.

Technology

Technology is viewed as another tool aiding cost-effective work while at the same time providing access to quality data for decision-making on a timely basis. Technology consists of hardware (personal computers, servers), network systems [wide area and local area networks (WAN and LAN) and software (computer applications and data base programs)]. The preferred approach to technology software is the use of best of breed business applications. Here the business applications that best meet the functions required to perform the business requirements are selected. An integrated technology solution is created through the use of interfaces. A number of interfacing methods are available to provide the flexibility required to match the quick pace of software product updates and releases.

Methods

The work procedures and maintenance practices are well documented in the CWMS. They are the optimal maintenance tactics derived from RCM evaluations. The output of the RCM process is an optimal mix of quality PM (with appropriate predictive maintenance and condition-based monitoring tasks), time based tasks and run-to-failure tasks. This approach ensures that work planning and scheduling done by the maintenance and operation work cells is cost effective.

Materials

There is good inventory management focused on optimal stores value, number of stock items and service level. There are properly managed satellite stores and centralized stores together with the appropriate mix of consignment and just-in-time (JIT) inventory management practices. The work management, inventory and purchasing functionality are seamlessly integrated into the CWMS to ensure that quality parts are always available for work order task scheduling and execution.

Services

There is an appropriate mix of services and internal work force for doing work where internal staffing is based on normal situations (demand) and outside services are used in the peak situations. The cost and quality of the work done by the outside services is closely monitored and controlled using the CWMS. It also provides a benchmark for the internal work force to try to meet and surpass. Every effort is made to have union approval of this approach to managing the workload.

Tools

There is an increased use of specialized tools associated with identifying potential failures and doing repairs before failure occurs. In addition, tools in good working condition are always available through use of a properly managed tool room using the CWMS. There is a culture of seeking out the latest ideas, innovations in tools and technology to work smarter and eliminate non-value-added activities.

Data

The work management process creates valuable data that is stored in the CWMS database. The computer hardware infrastructure allows all users easy access to this data. System users can routinely query the database via canned CWMS reports or create ad hoc reports using a report writer. This gives users much needed information for decision making with respect to day-to-day activities and also can be used to drive the medium and long-term plans. Information can be used to initiate continuous improvement projects that directly impact equipment and improve asset reliability. This information can also identify key improvement initiatives that can drive the capital project program.

THE WORK MANAGEMENT PROCESS

The work management process is executed more regularly than any other business process industry. It has been verbally done in the past without any documentation and has been paper based (work order templates with numerous copies that are filed physically in folders or on cabinets). Workflow is the framework that holds all the components together. In its simplest form this can be verbal approval to proceed with work scheduling and execution or can be very complex with approvals, security restrictions and messaging. With the advent of high-speed computers, complex programs and massive data storage capacity the work management process can be very automated. Figure 2.2 shows the eight components (including workflow) of the work management process. These are discussed in detail below and are discussed further in Chapter 4 in the context of the CWMS.

Work Initiation

Work can be initiated in many ways. This can be from equipment fail-

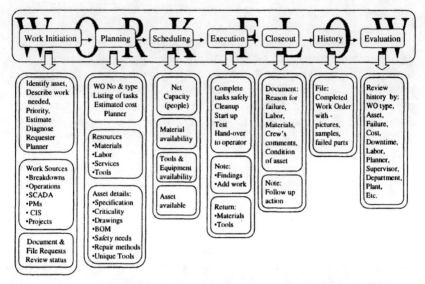

FIGURE 2.2 The Work Management Process.

ures (identified by operations or maintenance), facilities and equipment upgrades, safety or environmental concerns, preventive maintenance (PM) that is due, customer requests or aesthetic improvements. It is expected that the work requester indicate verbally or in writing what is required (describing the asset, the problem, the account to charge), what is the diagnosis of the problem, how important is the request and how soon should it be addressed. Usually the requester files a copy of the request before sending it off to the party responsible for addressing the request. The work request now becomes part of the Work Request backlog. The initiator will regularly inquire about the status of this request (sometimes identified by a number) depending on the importance of the work order task.

Work Planning

The request created by the initiator eventually finds its way to the person who is responsible for planning the work order task. Workflow parameters would dictate how quickly the request reaches its final destination and how quickly it sees some action. At this stage, the planner can either plan the work order task from scratch or, as is usually the case in most industries, use a previous work order task as a template. This is the stage where the work request becomes a work order. The planner needs the details about the asset to be worked on [criticality, specifications, safety/environmental (permit) requirements], work methods applicable to the asset and spares and services typically used in repairs. The detailed tasks, based on the work methods, can then be developed with the appropriate labor, material (materials, tools and special equipment) and services needed to execute the task. At this stage the planner has a good estimate of how much the entire work order task would cost and can seek an approval to proceed using workflow. Once approved, the work order becomes active and joins the other work orders in the work order backlog. At the same time, all materials are ordered through stores check out requests (or material requisitions) for items stocked in the stores. Any non-stores or services items are ordered through a purchasing system. Workflow plays an important role at this phase in order to meet policy guidelines on spending limitations.

Work Scheduling

Scheduling of work orders is the process of identifying which work order tasks will be done, when they will be done and by which crew and/or employees. A work order can be scheduled to be done on a specific day and time with a 100% surety only if all scheduling elements are in place. For this phase to be effective it is important that all materials, services, tools, special equipment and labor (commonly referred to as net capacity) are available together with the availability of the asset for which the work is to be done. If any of these scheduling elements are not in place then the work order or task cannot be done and there will be consequential non-value-added time associated with waiting while efforts are made to resolve the problem. Workflow is the framework that ensures all these elements are in place before a work order is scheduled. The result of scheduling efforts is a list or lists of work order tasks (with relevant details such as tasks, permits and drawings) that will be done by crews or individuals on a specific day, week or month.

Work Execution

Once a work order is scheduled, workers can proceed with the execution phase by collecting materials, tools and equipment, arranging "lock out and tag out" or other permitting requirements and proceed with doing the various tasks. During the actual work execution there needs to be access to information that was not provided (e.g., assembly drawings, clearances, torque values or different spares) to add or modify the tasks based on new information that becomes available. Tasks may be completed in a matter of hours or may continue for days and weeks. Noting work progress, completion and the crew's observations and findings during the repair or overhaul process are important aspects of the execution phase. This information is a vital step in optimizing the planning process for future work on the asset. Completion of the job should trigger certain workflow activities such as informing the requester that the job is completed.

Work Closeout

This is a component of the work management process that has been sadly lacking in most industries. Generally the focus is on doing the work as quickly as possible so as to be able to move on to another job. Any completion details or crew's comments are either not recorded or are limited to employee time charged to the work order. This is the component of the work management process that enables the optimization of work by providing an opportunity to capture valuable work history in addition to task detail and cost. The reason for failure, follow-up on work, descriptive details on failed components, photographs and videos are some of the ways to capture what happened.

Work History

All the data/information created directly or indirectly from the preceding components of the work management process can be valuable history for use in the evaluation phase. Generally, this information is stored as files that can be paper or electronic. The index system is usually based on the asset number by plant or facility or the responsible supervisor. Ideally, all relevant information is regularly added to these files to build the history of what work was done on the asset. It is important that the appropriate data is added and that there is quality control of the actual data provided.

Work Evaluation

The work evaluation component of the work management process is essential to provide feedback in the planning and scheduling components. On a day-to-day basis the planner needs to know if the right job plan was put together with accurate determinations of resources and time to do the actual task. If there is any variance the planner should be able to improve the accuracy of the planning function. Similarly, feedback on the actual findings from work done (closeout data) may dictate a change in the preventive maintenance frequencies for PM tasks. Data from predictive-type tasks would be useful in programming subsequent follow-up corrective work. Where a corrective work order was executed, closeout data can be useful in evaluation of the accuracy of the predictions from condition-monitoring tasks. Finally, it is always a good practice when planning and scheduling work to check on previous work done to identify failure trends and program upgrade or improvement-type work orders instead of repeating the same repair work as in the past.

Workflow

This is the final component of the work management process and is the framework that threads all the components together and provides the continuity and logical sequencing of events. In its simplest form workflow can be verbal approval to proceed with a work order and the purchase of goods and services. Workflow can, however, be much more complex with varying approval limits, use of substitute approvals, tracking of approval history, messaging to inform work requesters and planners of changes in the status of requests (work or purchasing) and budget checks before proceeding to another component. In most industries even complex workflow practices can be achieved manually through high staff levels (including clerical) and lots of paper records. As the volume of work increases, workflow is achieved at a premium price in high non-value-added staff costs, high waiting time, work delays and, most importantly, employee frustration and lack of confidence in the system. Employees see this as a tool to control them and sense of lack of trust.

THE CWMS IN BEST PRACTICES

The issues described above are resolved quite effectively by using the CWMS as a tool to execute the work management process. The CWMS is a key enabler of best practices, allowing electronic control of the work management process and at the same time providing an easy way to initiate, plan and schedule large volumes of work. Data collection, storage, easy access and evaluation are a major strengths of the CWMS. Operations and maintenance personnel (at all levels) can easily use the CWMS to take control of the work and, as a team, move from a reactive way of working to a proactive work environment. When the various best practices concepts such as RCM, PdM, TPM and performance management are introduced, the CWMS is the ideal vehicle to execute the work management process. The data collected in the process can be easily used to enable the continuous improvement process typical of the optimized work environment.

The CWMS further integrates the work management process with a number of support processes either seamlessly by supplying some of the support modules as part of the CWMS product or by the use of interfaces. The resulting integrated software product is a powerful business tool for doing work cost effectively, paying for goods and services, producing quality products and managing assets and employees. Figure 2.3 shows the various processes that impact the work management process. These include purchasing, inventory, accounts payables, capital projects, employee development (human resources), equipment operations (process control), payroll, production scheduling and asset life cycle management. The role of the CWMS in best practices, the work management and these support processes are discussed in detail in Chapters 4, 5 and 6.

Cost Reporting and Work History

The CWMS can be set up to track cost and work history at the asset and

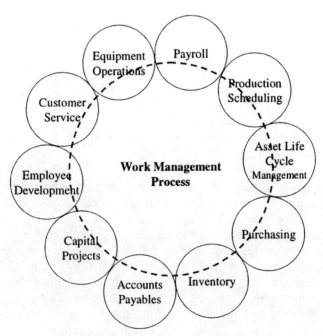

FIGURE 2.3 *Work Management and Support Processes.*

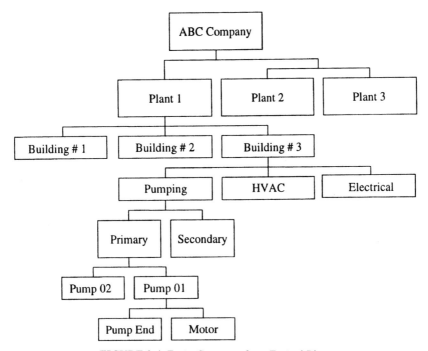

FIGURE 2.4 *Entity Structure for a Typical Plant.*

component level. At the higher levels work history is no longer relevant and the focus is more on cost. All other levels are therefore considered to be performance centers for tracking costs. Lower levels report to parents and the resulting structure is called the parent-child relationship or the entity hierarchy. (The term entity is generic and can represent a pump, pipe segment or equally represent a plant or department.) The parent-child relationship allows costs to be accumulated at individual entities and roll all the way up the structure to the parent entity. Figure 2.4 gives an example of an entity hierarchy in a typical plant environment.

By creating appropriate cost categories (e.g., labor, materials, services, total maintenance cost, total cost) it is possible to view the cost of work at any level in the structure based on budgeted, estimated, committed or actual figures. Figure 2.5 gives an example of a typical cost code structure to capture cost of doing work.

General ledger (GL) numbers, set up at the entity level, satisfy the accounting requirements for cost reporting as journal entries are created and posted for each transaction against these GLs on a regular basis. This is transparent to the CWMS user who looks at the cost of doing work at the entity level and as such does not have to be concerned about GLs. This type of work history and cost information at the fingertips of users can make an immediate positive impact in the decision-making process with respect to work management. Data on similar assets can be easily compared to identify strengths and weaknesses as well as establish standards where good practices have been identified. It is very popular and effective for people who are required to manage costs at the entity or asset level. A detailed discussion of the entity hierarchy is provided in Chapter 4.

Activity Based Costing Using a CWMS

Another aspect of cost tracking in the CWMS is the ability to do activity based costing (ABC). This is different from the typical entity-based costing discussed above in that it captures cost associated with doing work by the type of work being done. It is possible to create ABC codes that represent pump repairs or building repairs, HVAC repairs or conveyor overhauls. These codes can also be assigned to satisfy account reporting requirements. This type of information is very useful to senior management who may be interested in managing the operations at the macro level and would like to identify and control high-cost areas. In addition, they can easily compare similar operations at different plant sites and leverage good practices with a goal of standardization.

Asset Reliability Using a CWMS

Work management in an optimized work environment using the CWMS means extension of asset life by improving asset performance to meet the users' standards in a cost-effective and safe manner. The goal is

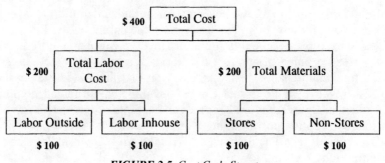

FIGURE 2.5 *Cost Code Structure.*

to minimize breakdowns on critical assets and increase the mean time between failure (MTBF), or reliability. The operations people can now plan for the use of these assets in the production of goods or delivery of services with a high degree of confidence that they would be available and be able to safely produce a quality product at the required rate. This is accomplished with the CWMS in three ways: executing the work management functionality using the various modules, creating and storing high quality data for evaluating asset performance and condition and enabling continuous improvement. The bottom line with improved asset reliability in an optimized work environment is a lean and competitive organization using highly reliable assets to produce goods or services.

Operations and Maintenance Using the CWMS

The traditional approach to work management was based on maintenance and operations working in silos. Operations were viewed as the people generatin work and maintenance was there to do the work. In this environment, the CWMS can be used to create and track work requests, make demands on inventory items as well as purchase goods and services to support operational work. Maintenance would use the CWMS to initiate maintenance identified work requests, plan and schedule all work as well as execute closeout work orders. The CWMS would also be used by maintenance to set up and manage a preventive maintenance program and procure goods (stores or non-stores) and services to support the work management process. In an optimized work environment, both operations and maintenance share the responsibility for the work management process. The team-based organization would share all components of the work management process based on the work that they do. As discussed earlier, operators would do work based TPM and the CLAIR concept. Maintenance would focus on core maintenance work order tasks as well as tasks designed to identify and correct potential failures before they occur. Both groups would have access to and use the data in the system to identify and implement improvement opportunities.

Roles of the Various Players Using the CWMS

The Work Initiator

Any person in the organization can initiate a work request. It can be the operator observing an unusual situation with an asset (noise, smell) or a clerical person who needs to have a desk repaired. After the work request has been dispatched electronically, the initiator can easily track the status of the request at any time.

The Planner

This is the person who is responsible for planning the details of the job. They would typically search for all requests addressed to him or her and either plan a job from scratch or copy an existing job and make suitable changes. For each task the planner will either create requisitions for services or items not available in stores or create a stores checkout request for those that are in stock. The planned job is then made active and sent to the work order backlog to be scheduled. In addition, the planner will manage the preventive maintenance program by triggering PM in the system on a regular basis. All PM that is due will automatically create a completely planned work order (previously set up in the system) with appropriate resource details.

The Scheduler

This person will coordinate the four scheduling elements using the CWMS. Work orders would only be scheduled if the labor, materials (including tools), services and the asset to be worked on were all in place. The CWMS can be configured to ensure that jobs cannot be scheduled unless these elements are in place. (Note that the planner scheduler role is usually covered by one job description in most organization.)

The Inventory Clerk

The inventory clerk will use the CWMS to issue stock items to workers against specific work order numbers, entities or account numbers. In addition, this person will receive materials on-line using the CWMS as well as assist in the inventory management process (e.g., physical counts).

The Warehouse Supervisor

The warehouse supervisor uses the CWMS to replenish the inventory by running the reorder report on a regular basis and reviewing the requisitions created before sending them to the buyer for action. In addition, the supervisor would conduct general inventory management such as physical counts, setup of new stock items and deletion of obsolete items. The warehouse supervisor would also make use of the data on stock items and transaction history to manage the warehouse effectively.

The Buyer

All requisitions end up in the buyer's backlog after being approved through workflow. The buyer can create a purchase order from scratch or by copying an existing one. In addition, the buyer can create a request for quotation to get the most competitive bid and either create a purchase order or set up a contract for the item(s). The buyer can also use the system to track the performance of the purchasing operations.

The Invoicing Clerk

The invoicing clerk can use the accounts payables function of the CWMS to enter vendor invoices and use the system to automatically match the invoice to purchase order and receiving information. Any unmatched invoices can be easily sent to the appropriate user for rectification of the problem (inventory clerk or buyer) or back to the vendor if necessary. All matched invoices are approved for payment and can be sent electronically to the financial system for payment.

The Maintenance Supervisor

This person may use the system to initiate work requests of purchase requisitions, however, they benefit most from the use of the data created and stored in the CWMS. The supervisor can monitor daily, weekly, monthly and annually the progress of his or he area of responsibility from reactive to proactive work. In addition, detailed evaluation of the data can yield valuable recommendations for improvements that can be the start of doing optimized work.

The Engineer

Like the supervisor, the engineer can use the data in the system to better design new processes and plants, or upgrade existing systems and improve performance. If the capital projects functionality is purchased with the CWMS, the engineer can actually initiate all projects within the CWMS and benefit from use of the inventory, purchasing and work order functions in the course of executing the project.

Senior Management (Operations, Maintenance)

Managers can monitor the operations on a daily, weekly, monthly and annual basis. They can advise and assist subordinates on how they could use the data in the CWMS to improve their operations. The data is also very helpful in decision making with respect to funding and budgets for new projects. Like their subordinates, they can easily track the progress of the operations from reactive to proactive work. They can also use the data to identify improvement opportunities. Most importantly, these senior managers can work together at their level using the CWMS to take the operations into an optimized way of working by encouraging and fostering a continuous improvement environment.

CHAPTER 3

How to Justify a CWMS for Your Business

IDENTIFYING THE NEED FOR A CWMS

Senior management tends to be focused on the bottom line and is not overly interested in any initiative or project that is not financially attractive. Decision makers look to tangible returns on any investment in line with the generally accepted economic criteria of net present value (or net present worth), return on investment (ROI) and payback period. These indicators can be developed for any project using the business case concept where dollar inflows (benefits) and outflows (costs) are modeled on a spreadsheet over the life of the project. The economic indicators are the key output from the business case. In order to develop a suitable CWMS project, it is essential to recognize and document the need for a CWMS. It is very easy to identify signs in your business that dictate the need for a CWMS. These signs can be at the macro level and can be further supported by more detailed evaluation. The following are some of the indicators to look for.

- High equipment downtime—These are usually the easiest records to come by because equipment downtime is directly related to production or service and is usually tracked closely by senior management. Equipment downtime can be categorized by two areas: (1) Downtime can be due to operational or process problems and is also due to changeovers. (2) Downtime can be due to maintenance repairs (proactive or reactive). This is useful information in justifying a CWMS. Sometimes this data is viewed differently as equipment uptime, i.e., the percentage of time that the equipment is available for use. This should be in the range of 95–100%, depending on the industry.

- High percentage of reactive work/high maintenance cost—Reactive work encompasses breakdown maintenance, corrective maintenance (that can be planned) due to secondary damage from breakdowns as well as any other unplanned work. Reactive work is also characterized by very little planning and scheduling, poor support from inventory and purchasing, a very high work order backlog and a high cost of maintenance (labor, services and materials). There is a high degree of non-value-added work such as waiting for materials, tools, availability of equipment for work to be done, excessive traveling, wrong parts and inaccurate assessment of the work to be done. The ideal balance of reactive to proactive work should be 25% to 75% respectively.
- Poor preventive maintenance program—A poor PM program is a good indicator that a CWMS can be beneficial to your organization. Inadequate PM and/or poor quality PM, together with very low PM compliance, are sure signs that the work force is struggling to take control of the maintenance of assets.
- Asset reliability (mean time between failures)—Low asset reliability, indicated by very frequent failures (small interval between failures), is another indication that the work force is not in control of the maintenance operations. There is usually a lot of repetitive high cost failures that are easily forgotten in the daily panic and fire-fighting mode of operating.
- Relationship between operations and maintenance—High conflict between operations and maintenance is an another indication that there is an urgent need to take control of the work and maximize the performance of the assets. There is general feeling of frustration and inability to change things.
- Poor inventory and purchasing control and management—This is characterized by poor stores service level (<95%), high numbers of stock items but also high numbers of stock outs, long lead times for replenishment of the inventory, low inventory turnover ratios (<1.5) and high inventory value. A CWMS can be helpful where there is high inventory losses or inability to account for items used. Also, poor purchasing support is characterized by a lack of confidence in the buyers due to long waits for non-stores and services purchase orders, poor quality items and an unwillingness by the purchasing group to listen to the needs of operations and maintenance.

- Little or no records—The inability to find asset work and cost records, documentation on PM and work order closeout information are sure signs that a CWMS can be very helpful. This can even be as bad as lack of inventory records or unreliable records.
- Safety and the environment—A high number of safety issues or violations of regulatory standards is typical of a reactive way of working. A CWMS can provide the means to take control of the operations and reduce or eliminate this unacceptable situation.
- High overtime and staffing levels—The typical reaction to dealing with an out-of-control work situation is to throw money and people at it. This can mean high overtime to complete work and get equipment back into production and paying premium dollars for much needed spares or services or to replace complete components or pieces of equipment. In addition, there is a tendency to overstaff the maintenance and operations groups at all

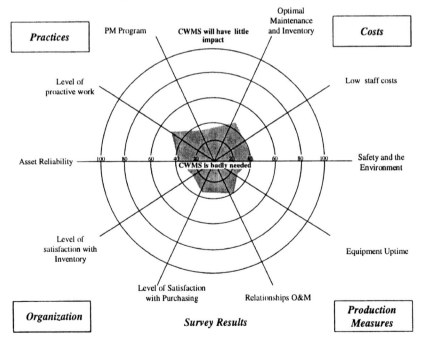

FIGURE 3.1 *Self Evaluation on CWMS Needs.*

levels to manage the out-of-control situations that tend to be the norm instead of the peaks.

These indicators can be represented graphically in a radar diagram format to visually show the need for a CWMS. An example of an assessment that shows there is compelling need for a CWMS is given in Figure 3.1.

The previously mentioned areas are good high-level indicators of a work environment that can benefit substantially from a CWMS. An evaluation at that level can be easily conducted within a few days to identify if there is a need to continue with the process to justify a CWMS. If the indicators are very compelling it is important at this stage to seek a champion for the CWMS effort at a senior level in management. This can be the maintenance manager, the operations manager or the person responsible for both groups. It should be noted that in some circles there is no need to do any evaluation because a CWMS is considered to be an absolute necessity for competitiveness in today's industry. A CWMS is viewed as a critically needed tool for office productivity, financial and human resources systems, e-mail and voice mail.

DEFINING THE REQUIREMENTS FOR A CWMS

Once the overall need for a CWMS has been established and there is approval to proceed with a more detailed evaluation it is important that the requirements for the CWMS are defined so as to develop costs for the cost-benefit analysis. This step requires the creation of a small team of up to six people to conduct the evaluations and subsequent business case for the CWMS. Team members should be from various disciplines (maintenance, operations, inventory, purchasing, information technology and engineering). It is usually a good idea to select a team leader who has an overall grasp of the company's operations. The following are necessary to define the CWMS requirements and also capture the relevant cost details.

Interviews

Conduct candid interviews with personnel (supervisory and frontline) in the maintenance, operations, purchasing and inventory areas. Also, it can be quite revealing to interview key members of senior management, including the operations, maintenance, inventory, purchasing and engineering managers, the companys' financial officer and general manager.

Interviews should try to flush out the concerns that people have with the work management process, the cost of doing work, the reliability of the assets, the relationships of individual sections and the general level of satisfaction with the support services to the work management effort.

Existing Level of Technology

It is important that the team understands the existing technology environment in the company. This should include details on all the existing business applications, databases, data records, networking and hardware infrastructure. System performance, limitations of existing applications and interfaces and quality of data are very useful to the evaluation effort. The IT member of the team can easily acquire this information. This data can be very critical to any decisions on replacing an existing CWMS with a new CWMS.

Existing Benchmark Information and the Quality of Existing Data

It is important that the team documents key benchmarks for the critical information. This is critical to analyzing the gap in desired versus existing performance. Here the focus should be on

- cost indicators
  —material, labor and services cost associated with doing work, cost of paper and forms, energy, projects (stores material and internal labor costs)
  —equipment uptime or downtime and cost impact on production
- level of reactive work versus proactive or optimized work
  —PM compliance
  —quality of PM
  —level of predictive work
  —average work request backlog
  —average work order backlog
  —number of repeat jobs for the same problem
  —equipment reliability
  —overall equipment effectiveness
- material management indicators
  —inventory turnover
  —value of the inventory
  —number of obsolete or slow-moving items
  —number of stock outs

      —number of incorrect or poor quality parts or components
      —number of purchase orders
      —contracts or blanket purchase order
      —cost per PO of purchasing services
      —average time to process a PO from the requester identifying the
         need to actual placement of the PO
- employee indicators
      —overtime
      —sick leave
      —number of workmen's compensation cases
      —level of absenteeism
- safety and regulatory issues or violations
- staffing levels (supervisory and front line for all groups)

Observing Work Practices

The team should provide time in their schedule to observe all the key work practices and identify the value-added and non-value-added steps in the process. The planning and scheduling of jobs, job execution, inventory and purchasing processes are key processes to be reviewed. This can prove to be a good opportunity to have frank discussions with the people who are responsible for doing work. Some effort should be made to allocate time frames to the various activities being observed as discretely as possible (without making people feel they are being measured).

Defining the "As Is" Work Processes

In order to define the functional requirements for the CWMS the team should first try to understand how work is presently being done in the company. To do this, a detailed mapping of the existing business processes has to be conducted. All efforts should be made to identify the steps in each process and the different players involved in the steps. The data collected from the previously described efforts is very useful in this activity. In addition, it may be necessary to invite the people who are actually involved in the processes to participate in the mapping exercise. This activity can be documented using flip charts and post-it notes to define the process flow. It can also be done quite effectively using the computer with a process-mapping tool, such as Visio, and a data projection system. The final result should be a detailed process map for each of the key business processes together with notes on who is involved in each step, the estimated time and cost to do it and any other relevant information. It is important to note any "hand off" from steps that lead to other processes. For example, in the work planning process there will be a hand off to the inventory or purchasing process for the procurement of materials (stock or non-stock) and services necessary to do the job.

The following business processes (with their associated workflow steps) are useful in this analysis:

- work management process (normal)
  —work initiation
  —planning
  —work assignment and scheduling
  —work closeout
  —work evaluation
  —reports
- work management process for emergency work
- preventive maintenance
  —creating PM
  —linking PM to assets
  —creating the PM forecast as PM due
  —PM reporting
- safety work process
  —creating and managing work related permits (lock and tag out, confined space entry, hot work and other permits)
  —material safety data sheets (set up and management)
- budgeting process
  —budget creation
  —budget approval
  —budget management
- inventory process
  —receipt of goods
  —returns to the vendor
  —vendor management
  —storage
  —stock check out requests and issues
  —picking process and transfers
  —returns to stock
  —physical adjustments
  —inventory replenishment
  —reports
- purchasing process
  —initiating a purchase requisition
  —quotations

—creating and modifying purchase orders
—contracts (blanket purchase orders)
—expediting purchase orders
—closing out purchase orders
—vendor management
- accounts payables—invoicing process
    —entering vendor invoices
    —matching invoices against receipt and purchase order information
    —resolving unmatched invoices
- projects (operating budget as well as investment budget)
    —project initiation
    —project creation and budget development and approval
    —project execution and closeout
- records and documentation setup
    —new assets
    —new stock items
    —new vendors
    —safety and regulatory information

Designing the New Way of Working—"To Be" Business Processes

The activities associated with the definition of the "as is" business process are usually very interesting and by the end of the process people are amazed at the ineffective, non-value-added and costly steps in the process. People would be very anxious to jump in and redesign all the processes. However, the redesign process must however be structured and should be based on best practices principles, an organization design that enables empowerment of employees and the best technology solution that can support the desired value-added processes. In addition, the redesign solutions must be practical and should consider the company's unique industry, work culture and operating environment. The design of the "to be" processes can be done similar to what has been discussed perviously using flip charts or the computer. In evaluating each process, it is important that the following principles or concepts be applied:

- Eliminate all obvious non-value-added steps.
- Ensure that the people doing the work are the most important people in the organization and all others provide a support function in order that work can be done cost effectively.
- Create effective work teams with a proper mix of skills in order to reduce the number of people involved in the process.

- Consider a program to multiskill trades so as to reduce the number of people who have to work on particular jobs.
- Consider a full day's work for each person.
- Staff for the normal operation and import (overtime for staff or use of contractors) for the peak conditions.
- Redesign and/or automate processes to facilitate unattended operations.
- Empower employees and teams and design a supervisory structure that supports empowerment (less supervisory layers).
- Use technology (CWMS) to eliminate or reduce the effort and time involved in steps.
- Use technology to make workflow, data capture, storage and access as effective as possible.
- Consider centralized, decentralized or a mixture of both for location of work crews.
- Consider centralized, decentralized or a mixture of both for inventory management and support.
- Consider the use of the following purchasing practices:
  —preferred vendor arrangements (blanket orders and contracts)
  —just in time purchasing (JIT)
  —vendor consignment (where the vendor is responsible for keeping the shelves in the company's stores stocked at all times and owns the stock until it is used)
  —auto faxing, electronic data integration (EDI)
  —credit card purchases up to a certain dollar limit
- Approve electronically through work flow and more realistic approval levels.
- Use appropriate hardware and networking infrastructure to provide information to anyone in the company who needs it.
- Use new or modified tools and equipment so that people can work smarter and reduce the time taken to do a job safely.
- Consider a change in culture that encourages use of electronic information displayed on a screen or forwarded to another user through e-mail instead of creating numerous copies for circulation and filing.

The resulting design of the "to be" business processes should be documented with two major objectives in mind. First, the functional requirements of each of the key and support business processes for the CWMS can now be defined in detail. This would also include details on the necessary interfaces to other business applications to support the new way of working based on the use of a CWMS as part of an integrated solution.

Second, the documentation should clearly define the reduction in steps and numbers of people involved for each process. This should include the anticipated savings as well as the cost of changes that are recommended. The concepts and principles applied in the design to achieve the desired improvements should also be defined. Proper documentation will enable the team to create the business plan required to justify a CWMS for the operations.

THE BENEFITS AND SAVINGS THAT CAN BE REALIZED

The benefits can be divided into two categories: tangible benefits and intangible benefits associated with use of the CWMS to move from reactive to proactive and eventually to an optimized way of working. The following discussion provides some explanation of the anticipated savings and also provides an estimated range of savings based on the experience of the author as well as documentation by various other writers on maintenance management.

Tangible Benefits (Using the CWMS to move from Reactive to Proactive to Optimized Work)

Increased Asset Uptime

Control of the work backlog and the preventive maintenance program will allow the company to improve asset *uptime* by *10–30%*. This can be 10% in the first year of system implementation, 20% in the second year and 30% in the third year and 30% thereafter on an annual basis.

Reduced Material Costs

Less failure and better inventory management will yield a *savings of 10–30%* of the annual material cost associated with doing work. This can be 10% in the first year of system implementation, 20% in the second year and 30% in the third year and 30% thereafter on an annual basis.

Reduced Inventory Value

The actual number of stock items and the average quantities stocked can be reduced to optimal levels based on good inventory management practices using the CWMS. There would be better management of the addition of new stock items, removal of obsolete, slow moving items and optimal ROPs, ROQs and safety stock levels. The associated inventory value reduction can range from *5–15%* of the existing value of the inventory. In the first year of system implementation there can be 5% savings, followed by 10% in the second year and 15% thereafter on an annual basis.

Reduced Labor Costs

Planning and scheduling—Good planning and scheduling of work using the CWMS, together with the reduction of non-valued-added time such as waiting and delays. can free up at least 5% of the maintenance work force in the second year of implementation. This can further improve to 10% per year by the end of the third year and 20% per year after.

Inventory and purchasing management—The CWMS can enable control of inventory and purchasing practices (with the elimination of the non-value-added activities and use of JIT, consignment and preferred vendor arrangements). This can translate into a staff reduction in both these areas by 10% in the second year and 20% per year after the third year of implementation.

Overtime—Overtime can be reduced by 5% in the first year, 10% in the second year and 15% per year after the third year of implementation. Overtime tends to be minimal after the third year of implementation of the CWMS.

Absenteeism—Absenteeism can be reduced by 5% per year due to better control of the work, less emergency and poorly planned jobs, less safety issues and less stressed employees.

Capital Projects

There can be a savings on capital projects (due to better planning, procurement of materials and services, use of internal resources, use of existing cost and work history on similar assets for design) from 5% in the second year of implementation to 7% per year after the third year of implementation.

Energy Costs

Increased equipment reliability and efficiency can reduce the average power required to start and operate motors or engines used to power equipment. Increased equipment availability can provide the flexibility to operate additional equipment during off-peak periods. This can all translate into energy savings from 5% in the second year to 10% per year after the third year of implementing the CWMS.

Paper Costs

The existing hardware, networking infrastructure and software available today can allow people to work in a paperless world if they are so inclined. Databases are regularly backed up and data can be properly secured and made available to anyone quite easily. Work requests, orders, requisitions, material check-out requests are all available electronically. Auto faxing, EDI, e-mail, and the Internet (e-commerce) can facilitate business with vendors without having to print purchase orders, invoices and checks. Reports can be run and be sent to numerous people as an attachment to e-mail. However, people take time to change and will not ever fully accept a paperless world. Overall stationery costs can be reduced from 20% in the first year to 30% in the second year and 40% per year after the third year of implementing the CWMS.

Continuous Improvement Projects

Good quality data captured by the CWMS can be a key source of information for initiating improvement projects in the operations. These can be related to workflow and can result in more cost-effective practices or can be related to asset replacement decisions based on cost and work history captured on assets. Overall, these projects can realize an average savings of 5% per year on operations and maintenance costs and can be realized from the third year after implementation.

Intangible Benefits

Moving from a reactive way of working to a proactive and eventually an optimized way of working using a CWMS provides some intangible benefits that can go a long way to selling a CWMS project to senior management. The following are some of the key benefits in this area.

- better staff motivation and commitment
- better trained staff
- a work culture that embraces change and smarter ways of working using technology (this makes it easier to make future changes)
- reduced or zero safety and environmental issues
- proper documentation of work plans for assets, cost and work

TABLE 3.1 Tangible Benefits from Implementing a CWMS.

Benefit	Cost savings (% of annual associated cost)									
	Yr 1	Yr 2	Yr 3	Yr 4	Yr 5	Yr 6	Yr 7	Yr 8	Yr 9	Yr 10
Tangible										
Asset uptime		10	20	30	30	30	30	30	30	30
Material cost (Work)		10	20	30	30	30	30	30	30	30
Inventory value		5	10	15	15	15	15	15	15	15
Labor										
Planning & scheduling		5	15	20	20	20	20	20	20	20
Inventory & purchasing		5	10	20	20	20	20	20	20	20
Overtime	5	10	15	15	15	15	15	15	15	15
Absenteeism	5	5	5	5	5	5	5	5	5	5
Capital projects		5	7	7	7	7	7	7	7	7
Energy costs		5	10	10	10	10	10	10	10	10
Paper	20	30	40	40	40	40	40	40	40	40
Continuous improvement (O&M)			5	5	5	5	5	5	5	5

history; for continuity when workers move on to other departments or retire and for supporting ISO 9000 requirements
- more reliable assets providing greater flexibility for the sales and production staff in meeting market demands and changes
- good quality information available to everyone for day-to-day decision making as well as to support continuous improvement initiatives
- good quality data on assets to support cost effective management of asset life cycle
- corporate knowledge retention

The above benefits are summarized in Table 3.1.

COSTS ASSOCIATED WITH SELECTING AND IMPLEMENTING A CWMS

There are numerous costs associated with a CWMS project. These can be direct investments at the beginning of the project, additional injection of funds at specific stages of the implementation, annual maintenance and system support costs as well as the use of internal resources. It is extremely important that all these costs are properly identified and estimated to develop a realistic business plan. This can range from $100,000–500,000 based on the time the consultants are on-site. This is a cost that can be minimized if the concepts discussed in this book are used to manage the project.

Direct Costs

Consulting costs to select and implement the CWMS—Many companies feel that they are incapable of managing this type of project due to lack of specific expertise, availability of resources and the need to focus on the core work on a day-to-day basis. As such, many companies turn to consulting firms for help and the cost of these services has to be accounted for in developing the business plan.

Software licensing costs—Software vendors make their profits through the sale of licenses of the various products. These licenses are usually based on the number of concurrent users that are signed on and are using the product. If the company has a large enough user base, it may qualify for a site license. A site license requires the company to pay for licenses up to a specific number (this can vary by vendor from 100–500); any additional licenses beyond the site license number are at no charge to the company. This is usually an attractive option for companies with a large user base and a high number of plants or divisions. The direct costs associated with the software licenses are paid when they are actually needed and bought.

Hardware and networking infrastructure upgrade costs—There is usually a major investment in hardware and networking infrastructure to match the requirements of the CWMS server and work station needs. This is usually a good opportunity to include upgrades that will allow other applications to operate more effectively and provide accessibility to everyone who needs them. Usually there are costs associated with new servers, work stations, upgrading the local area network (LAN), wide area network (WAN), mobile and remote computing requirements.

Implementation costs—In addition to the consulting costs listed above, there are other implementation costs that must be factored into the project costs. These are costs associated with definition, development and testing of the necessary interfaces to other applications; conversion of existing electronic data; system configuration, testing, documentation, end-user training and system roll out. These costs are usually split between the consulting firm and the vendor. However, this is an area in which company can save significant funds if the implementation method employed provides for early transfer of knowledge to internal resources and a reduction of the dependence on consulting support. This will be discussed in more detail in Chapters 9 and 10.

Write-off costs associated with an existing system—If there is an existing system that is being replaced, the cost associated with writing off this system must be considered in developing the business plan.

Internal resources—A CWMS project requires considerable investment of the time of valuable internal resources. They can be involved in functional requirements and business case development, system selection and implementation. If they are replaced when they provide their services to the project, the cost of the replacement should be considered. However, many companies are able to do without the services of these individuals for the duration of the project through temporary organizational changes and people taking on additional workloads. This is usually an indication that there is some fat in the organization anyway.

Annual Costs

System maintenance and support costs—All CWMS vendors provide maintenance and support services for their products to ensure that their clients stay current on the changes in the product; they also help with configuration and user-related problems. However, this support is provided at a cost that varies from 15–20% (of the overall product license cost) per year after the first year of implementation.

Keeping current on the hardware—The annual cost of upgrading the hardware to keep current with the CWMS technology should also be factored in to the overall annual cost. This can be a small cost if the IT department has a strategic approach to management of the infrastructure and can be shared across the company with other computerized system users, e.g., production systems, accounting and HR systems.

CWMS labor support costs—When an integrated software solution is implemented in the operations, there is a need for daily support of the technology (software application, operating systems and interfaces, hardware and networking) as well as system configuration support (changes to user profiles, security, value lists, reports). At a minimum, there is a need for at least one IT person and one CWMS practices coordinator. The average burdened salary for these support staff should be considered in the business plan. Note that these people can be part of the implementation team and can be easily trained during the various stages of the implementation process.

Vendor user conference participation—Most reputable CWMS vendors have an annual conference where all clients are invited to provide input into upgrades to the software, share their experiences with other users as well as preview upcoming new product releases and upgrades. It is usually very strategic to have the two support personnel attend the conferences on an annual basis (as well as others in the organization) to keep current on the solution that the company uses while learning ways to use the CWMS more effectively. The costs here are associated with conference registration, travel, meals and hotel charges.

COST-BENEFIT ANALYSIS (DEVELOPING THE BUSINESS PLAN)

There is a significant outlay of precious capital dollars required to fund the selection and implementation of a CWMS. Usually there is stiff competition for the available capital dollars from people wanting to do plant upgrades, other information technology systems and various other projects. Senior management requires clear information to decide how the available funding can be assigned to maximize the return on investment. While intangible benefits are normally well received and appreciated, senior management, and especially the accounting group, look for tangible information. The typical information requested is based on project life that can vary from 5–10 years (10 years is usually a good period for a CWMS project). The following is an explanation of the various accounting parameters that are used to define economic feasibility of a project.

- Net present value (NPV) of the funds. This considers the time value of money and the calculation uses an assumed interest rate and calculates what the value of the overall cost and investment money would be in each year of the project.
- Pay back period (PBP). This is the point where the NPV is equal to zero. At this point, the overall expenditure is equal to the savings any additional savings; then results in an overall return on investment. That is, after the PBP there is literally a profit from the investment.
- Rate of return on the investment (ROI). This is one of the more popular parameters used to evaluate economic feasibility. The investment costs and savings are evaluated at an assumed interest rate and the ROI is computed over the project life. The ROI can be compared to the return on investment over a similar time frame in a financial institution.

Before the advent of office productivity tools, all the above calcula-

TABLE 3.2 Cost-Benefit Analysis for a Typical CWMS Project.

Benefit				Year							
Costs	1	2	3	4	5	6	7	8	9	10	Total ($)
Direct costs											
Consulting services	100,000	100,000	25,000	0	0	0	0	0	0	0	225,000
Software licences	100,000	500,000	100,000	0	0	0	0	0	0	0	700,000
Hardware/networking infrastructure	100,000	100,000	100,000	0	0	0	0	0	0	0	300,000
Implemention services	100,000	100,000	25,000	0	0	0	0	0	0	0	225,000
Internal resources	100,000	100,000	25,000	0	0	0	0	0	0	0	225,000
System write-off	100,000	0	0	0	0	0	0	0	0	0	100,000
Subtotal	600,000	900,000	275,000	0	0	0	0	0	0	0	1,775,000
Annual costs											
Software maintenance	0	80,000	15,000	33,750	33,750	33,750	33,750	33,750	33,750	33,750	331,250
Hardware update	0	0	0	50,000	50,000	50,000	50,000	50,000	50,000	50,000	350,000
Labor support	0	0	0	150,000	150,000	150,000	150,000	150,000	150,000	150,000	1,050,000
Vendor user conference	10,000	10,000	10,000	10,000	10,000	10,000	10,000	10,000	10,000	10,000	100,000
Subtotal	10,000	90,000	25,000	243,750	243,750	243,750	243,750	243,750	243,750	243,750	1,831,250
Total costs	610,000	990,000	300,000	243,750	243,750	243,750	243,750	243,750	243,750	243,750	3,606,250

(continued)

TABLE 3.2 (continined) Cost-Benefit Analysis for a Typical CWMS Project.

Benefit	Year										Total ($)
Savings	1	2	3	4	5	6	7	8	9	10	
Increased production due to asset uptime		50,000	150,000	300,000	300,000	300,000	300,000	300,000	300,000	300,000	2,300,000
Reduced material usage		75,000	150,000	300,000	300,000	300,000	300,000	300,000	300,000	300,000	2,325,000
Reduced inventory value		100,000	150,000	300,000	300,000	300,000	300,000	300,000	300,000	300,000	2,350,000
Reduced labor	50,000	75,000	100,000	200,000	200,000	200,000	200,000	200,000	200,000	200,000	1,625,000
Better amanagement of capital projects		50,000	75,000	125,000	125,000	125,000	125,000	125,000	125,000	125,000	1,000,000
Energy savings		50,000	75,000	100,000	100,000	100,000	100,000	100,000	100,000	100,000	825,000
Reduction in paper costs	1,500	3,000	5,000	5,000	5,000	5,000	5,000	5,000	5,000	5,000	44,500
Savings due to ongoing CI projects			100,000	100,000	100,000	100,000	100,000	100,000	100,000	100,000	800,000
Total savings	51,500	403,000	805,000	1,430,000	1,430,000	1,430,000	1,430,000	1,430,000	1,430,000	1,430,000	11,269,500
Net savings	-558,500	-587,000	505,000	1,186,250	1,186,250	1,186,250	1,186,250	1,186,250	1,186,250	1,186,250	7,663,250
NPV	-521,963	-1,034,671	-622,441	282,544	1,128,324	1,918,772	2,657,509	3,347,917	4,831,180	6,446,771	
Cum NPV	9,907,489										
ROI	61%										

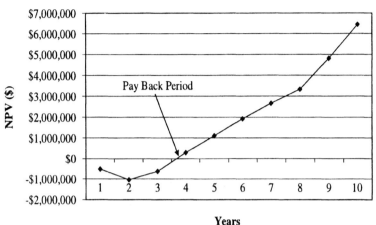

NPV for 10 yr CWMS Project

FIGURE 3.2 *Economic Analysis for a CWMS Project.*

tions were done manually. Today, all spreadsheet programs have these formulas available for calculating NPV and ROI. The PBP can be determined where NPV goes to zero or where the graph cuts the x-axis in a graphical plot. Each company may have varying values of pay back, NPV or ROI that would be considered worthwhile to proceed with the project. Table 3.2 gives an example of a cost-benefit analysis using an Excel spreadsheet and Figure 3.2 gives a graphical representation of the data in NPV data for each year in the project.

DEFINING THE CHALLENGES AND CONSTRAINTS

A CWMS project can be a risky undertaking and it is important that the challenges and constraints are clearly defined to aid senior management in their decision making. The following concerns should be understood and recommendations for addressing them should be prepared by the team.

- Managing change. A CWMS project is a major undertaking and requires changes to work practices as well as getting people to understand the benefits and readily embrace the technology. Open and honest communication at all stages in the project goes a long way to preparing people for change and creating a flexible organization that can easily make adjustments to changes.

- Interfacing new and existing technology. This is usually one of the more complicated and frustrating challenges that face the CWMS project team. A number of solutions for dealing with this problem are recommended in Chapter 6.
- Managing project costs. Project costs can be divided into two major categories: software and hardware costs and services cost. Software and hardware costs are heavily dependent on the up-front design and selection process and can be controlled. Services cost is more of a challenge because it encompasses costs associated with consultants hired to help with the selection and implementation process, vendor personnel who bring product-specific knowledge and expertise and internal resources. It is important in this area to maximize the use of internal resources and minimize the use of outside services through early transfer of knowledge to internal resources. This is discussed in more detail in Chapters 9 and 10.
- Achieving the benefits from the CWMS. The biggest risk in any project is the inability to achieve the benefits proposed in the business plan. A CWMS project can easily fall into this category. There must be a concerted focus on benefits tracking and the use of the CWMS as a tool to work more effectively and capture quality data that can be used for timely decision-making and continuous improvement projects. This is discussed in more detail in Chapter 11.
- Keeping current on the CWMS solution. A major concern of senior management is the rapid changes in technology that tend to make existing hardware and software obsolete in a few years. It is very important that the CWMS team selects and implements the system in a manner that caters for the advancements in technology. The key to managing this challenge is a good configuration and practices change management process. This will allow the company to easily implement software updates, patches, new releases and practices changes with minimal impact on the user population. In addition, it is very important that configuration data, work practices and procedures are well documented on a continuous basis. There should also be ongoing efforts at keeping all electronic data (work, cost history) updated and of high quality. This will enable the company to easily embrace any new technology that comes along without major impact on the operations. Chapter 12 provides good advice on this subject to people who are responsible for keeping the CWMS up to date.

- Other pitfalls to a CWMS project. There are a number of other issues and challenges that people should be aware of and know how to deal with when they come up. These are discussed in detail in Chapter 13.

PREPARING A WINNING CWMS PROPOSAL TO SENIOR MANAGEMENT

Having completed the cost-benefit analysis, the next major task is to prepare a winning proposal to senior management. In the example given in Table 3.2 and Figure 3.2 it is very obvious that investment of time and money in this project is a very profitable undertaking. However, this alone may not be enough to sell the project. It is important that the team clearly identifies the tangible as well as the intangible benefits. In addition, the challenges listed above should be clearly defined so that senior management can properly assess the benefits, costs and the risks associated with the project. There should be a clear demonstration by the team that they understand what is involved in the project and are prepared and capable of managing the various activities associated with the CWMS project and the various internal and external players. All of this data should be pulled together in a presentation that is simple, concise and flows smoothly from slide to slide. The typical presentation software (available in office productivity tools) and data projection system can go a long way to show that the team is willing to embrace technology and is capable of doing a great job. It is usually a good idea for the team to practice and have their sponsor critique the presentation beforehand. Obvious enthusiasm and excitement over the project can also demonstrate how passionate the team is about the project.

CHAPTER 4

CWMS Core Modules and Features

THE CWMS AND THE WORK MANAGEMENT PROCESS

The work management process is one of the oldest unchanged processes that is associated with almost every industry in the world today. Some industries have been very formal in conducting work using a very detailed documented process on one end of the scale as compared to companies on the other end of the scale as that conduct the work management process verbally and with little or no documentation. The basic work management process is shown in Figure 4.1 below and was discussed in detail in Chapter 2.

The CWMS is basically the software that enables execution of the work management process together with the associated business process of materials management. Materials management is tightly coupled to the work management process, because most jobs require the use of materials and/or services in order to get it done. Materials could either be from inventory or purchased from a vendor. Similarly, all services have to be purchased either from an external vendor or from an internal vendor (e.g., a machine shop). Interpretation of what constitutes work would also dictate how elaborate is the functionality that may be required. For example, if work includes capital projects then there should be a functionality that covers the unique requirement this area. All of these core modules work together through the Workflow module. This module essentially provides for the checks, controls and approvals necessary for effective work management. The following discussion takes the reader through the functionality typically found in each of these core modules.

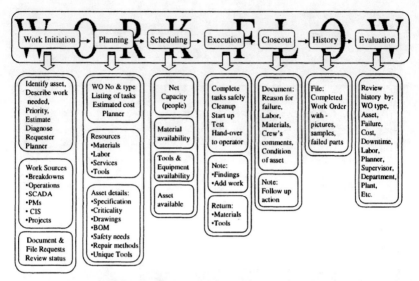

FIGURE 4.1 *The Work Management Process.*

In addition, some attention will be paid to identifying mandatory functionality that are critical to effective work management. (An example of a detailed list of functionality requirements for the core CWMS modules is given in Appendix 4.1).

KEY FUNCTIONALITY OF THE WORK ORDER MODULE (SOMETIMES REFERRED TO AS THE MAINTENANCE MODULE)

Work is always performed on an asset and as such it is important that assets can be set up in the system to allow work requests to be initiated by a user of the asset and different work orders be planned, scheduled and executed for the work identified. This module also provides the functionality for preventive maintenance (or proactive-type work such as regular overhauls, inspections, lubrications and checks). During the course of doing work it is important that both work and cost history are captured for the specific asset. We may desire to group the ongoing costs in a manner that allows people at all levels of the organization to monitor and control these costs. This has led to the concept of the hierarchy that shows the logical parent-child relationship for assets and performance centers discussed in Chapter 2.

ASSET RECORDS

These are usually the lowest level entity records in the hierarchy—work is done at this level. The system should provide the ability to allow the setup asset records that are uniquely identifiable. This is usually accomplished using entity numbers automatically allocated by the system or allowing the user to manually construct a smart number to match his existing numbering system. The asset record must allow the user to set up criticality, safety procedures, original equipment manufacturer information, specifications and drawings, bill of materials (spares and services normally required to do work on the asset), account numbers to capture cost of work done, owner of the asset, person who usually plans work for the asset and the statistics on asset condition that are usually collected on an ongoing basis to trigger preventive maintenance (PM) work or initiate work requests. The asset record should also provide the ability to link each asset record to unique documents, job plans, and PM that can be accessed from the asset record.

PERFORMANCE CENTERS

These are located higher up in the hierarchy and generally have one-to-one relationships to the business centers of the organizations. Costs roll up to these centers and "estimated, accrued and actual costs" are easily reported at any point as well as cumulated costs and can be compared in time to budgets. Sometimes the work is initiated at performance center levels when the history of the work is irrelevant (e.g., cleaning of washrooms, miscellaneous painting). Performance centers are also the best levels to set up account codes necessary to satisfy the financial accounting system requirements. The account numbers can then be duplicated to all children or when work is done at the asset level; the system will search up the hierarchy until it finds a parent with a valid account number.

WORK-RELATED FUNCTIONS

Work Request (WR)

This should provide functionality to enable execution of the steps shown in Figure 4.1 and as discussed in Chapter 2. Any authorized user should be able to locate the asset (or performance center—if the history of the work to be done is not relevant) and create a manual work request (WR) to initiate the process. The asset information should automatically be defaulted into the WR screen. The work requestor should then enter the description of the problem, the WR type, the interpretation of the failure symptom, the date by which the work should be done and then with one click of the mouse send it off to the next person in the process. This could either be an approving authority or a planner. The WR is now part of the WR backlog. Date, time and user identification should be automatically defaulted on the WR based on sign-on information. A request to do work is not necessarily valid work for the organization; it is only after approval that it becomes a legitimate part of the WR backlog. WRs can be created automatically when process control systems send information to the CWMS indicating alarm or fault conditions.

Work Orders (WO)

The respective planners will draw from this backlog, assess the work to be done (based on experience or actual visit to the job site) and create work orders (WO) either with a simple plan (one task) or very sophisticated work plans. Information from the asset record (specifications, bill of materials, safety procedures, standard jobs) are unique features that allow easy planning. WOs can be created automatically when PMs reach their trigger points (triggers could be time-, calendar-, statistic-, event-based or can be a combination of any of these.

Planning

When WOs are planned, the cost of the work to be done is more accurate. It may be necessary to go through another level of approval if there are budget restrictions or limited funds before the WO can go into the WO backlog ready for scheduling. During the course of planning, electronic reservations may be made for items in inventory and/or electronic purchase requisitions (PRs) can be initiated and sent to the relevant buyers.

Scheduling

Scheduling of the active WOs in the backlog requires the ability to match labor resources, track material, services tools and equipment availability together with release of the asset by operations to allow work to be done. The scheduler (planning and scheduling is usually combined into one job description in most organizations) requires the ability to create a schedule by crew, individual employee and the ability to sequence WO and WO tasks through a two-way link to project management software. When a WO is scheduled, the WO is assigned a crew or person, the date and time for work execution is identified, and all resources to do the job are arranged to be available on the scheduled date.

Work Execution

This requires functionality in the CWMS to track work in progress as well as allow employees to charge their time to the WO or WO task until it is completed. In the case of jobs of short duration this is not necessary and the job is completed without any further interaction with the CWMS until it is time to Closeout the WO or WO task.

WO Closeout

This is a key work management functionality that is usually treated with little importance. The CWMS should allow for text entry of any unique findings relevant for work history, digital photos, failure codes necessary for history evaluation, materials and services used, asset statistics and any recommended follow-up work with a linked WR created when the WO or WO task is closed. All closed WOs should be placed in a history file for access during the evaluation phase.

WO Evaluation

Work execution is typically accomplished by flexible reporting functionality. A CWMS should provide the ability to query the WO history database based on user-defined criteria to extract data relevant to the task at hand—this may be reviewing of history when planning work on the asset or evaluating similar failures across a cross section of assets. WO evaluation is critical to continuous improvement and work optimization.

CAPITAL PROJECTS-RELATED FUNCTIONALITY

This functionality is really work management on a much larger scale than that discussed previously and is usually associated with the creation of new assets, major upgrades or modifications to existing assets. (Some CWMS vendors do not provide unique functionality for capital projects and suggest that this can be done through their WO module.) Actual work execution can be done through the purchasing module by letting of major contracts with individual tasks managed from project management software. In addition, work can be done through the creation of work orders that can be executed with internal resources. It is important that the CWMS provides the ability to create projects and subprojects each with its unique account code. The budgets for these subprojects roll up to the project header level to create the overall budget for the project. The system should allow for the approval cycle and the creation of an approved active project. During the execution phase of the project, any asset-related information for assets created should populate the asset record with the asset in an inactive status. Commissioning sets the stage for transfer of ownership to the O&M group with all information, as identified earlier in this chapter, in place and available to support the work management process.

MATERIALS MANAGEMENT (THE INVENTORY AND PURCHASING MODULES)

Having the right materials and services available, on time, and of the right quality and specifications, is the ultimate goal for materials management in the support of work management. This can be achieved by the right balance of on-site stocking or timely purchase from suitable vendors. CWMS functionality should provide seamless access to each of these modules from the work order module during the planning phase for WOs. This would require automatic reservations of stock items and the creation of pick lists for items to be staged for the work order at the stores or electronic requisitions to buyers for the goods and services to be purchased from vendors. In addition, each module should provide the necessary functionality to support the key inventory and purchasing function.

INVENTORY FUNCTIONALITY NEEDED TO SUPPORT THE INVENTORY CYCLE (FIGURE 4.2)

The inventory module should allow setup of all necessary stores records required for effective inventory management. These include the item record (the most important), setup of different warehouses, setup of receiving locations, and setup of the various stores personnel with the varying level of authorities. In general, the system should allow one to set up all the details currently needed for standard inventory control. The

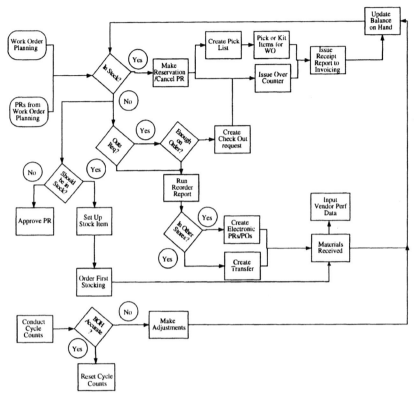

FIGURE 4.2 *The Inventory Cycle.*

item record is discussed in some more detail here. Full details of the remaining functionality are given in Appendix 4.1.

Item record detail incluces stock item number, classification, description, MSDS data, when linked to a warehouse; then balance on hand, reorder point (ROP), reorder quantity (ROQ), stock safety level, storage requirements, price, vendor and location information (row, aisle, bin) is necessary.

Inventory transactions are key to enabling the inventory cycle. The system should allow receipt of stock (allowing for the entry of vendor performance statistics), issues to support work orders (including consignment items), returns to stock of material not used, transfers between warehouses, support for cycle counting and physical adjustments and automatic/manual reorder of items reaching the ROP with the creation of either electronic PRs or POs.

PURCHASING FUNCTIONALITY NEEDED
TO SUPPORT THE CYCLE
(FIGURE 4.3)

Like the inventory functionality, the system should also support the setup of all the relevant records to support the purchasing cycle. These include the PR, PO, vendor (ordering and payment), buyer, request for quotation (RFQ) and contract. The system should also provide support for all the key purchasing functions: creation of PRs, conversion of PRs to either POs or RFQs, bid analysis and contract award, expediting, vendor and buyer performance evaluation. In some systems the three-way matching process for comparing the PO to what is received in stores against the PO and the vendor's invoice is considered a purchasing functionality and is included in the purchasing module. Full details of the remaining functionality are given in Appendix 4.1.

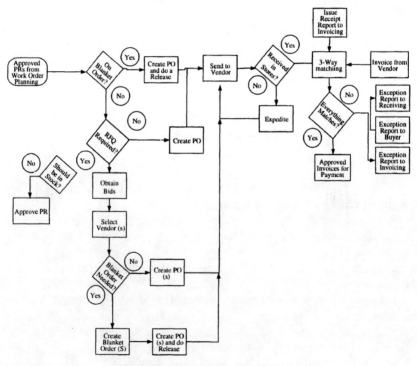

FIGURE 4.3 *The Procurement Cycle.*

WORKFLOW

This is considered to be the engine of the CWMS and provides the framework and functionality to enable the workflow process. Essentially, this should allow for a central work place (workflow headquarters) through which all actions, messages, special reports and functionality of the various modules is located. In this regard, workflow should provide for electronic approvals (manual or automatic) based on user-defined criteria, send automatic messages when key events occur prompting the user to carry out a specific action and send e-mail messages (again manual or automatic) needed to support the work process. Full details of the remaining functionality are given in Appendix 4.1.

ASSET MANAGEMENT

Effective asset management depends on collection, screening and evaluation of vast amounts of data in order to make decisions related to the asset at various stages in its life cycle. This data can be finance-, work-, operations-, maintenance- and condition-related (e.g., data needed to plot deterioration curves). An integrated technology solution supports asset management. There are two core business applications necessary for effective asset management: computerized work management system (CWMS) and an asset management system (AMS). The integrated technology solution requires the development of appropriate interfaces and links between the CWMS and other business applications such as financial and administrations systems (FAS), geographical information systems (GIS), SCADA/process control, pavement management systems, predictive maintenance systems (PdM) and closed circuit television (CCTV) in order to do effective work management on the asset. Data captured in this process can then feed an asset management system for plotting of deterioration curves, economic modeling and development of the capital project plans that will then be executed in the CWMS. This data will also be the source for creating the necessary reports to manage performance and provide proof of regulatory compliance (e.g., GASB 34 reports). The asset management system should also be able to provide an integrated view of assets. For example, in the public works environment, one should be able to see the condition of the pavement, water line, and sewer line for a particular segment of street. Any improvement plan should be considered for the overall integrated asset when modeling is carried out. Some major challenges that must be resolved in the development of an enabling integrated technology solution are: maintaining the integrity of the asset record, especially where it is shared by many different systems; developing a common asset numbering system and achieving an appropriate balance for real time, near real time and batch data transfer.

PERFORMANCE MANAGEMENT

The saying, "What gets measured gets done" is a key driver for a CWMS. In the course of doing work there is significant data that can be collected to provide a focus on the corporate and departmental goals and objectives. A CWMS should allow for easy data collection and retrieval. In this regard, there should be flexibility to add user-defined fields in addition to the standard fields provided by the vendor to capture data unique to your organization. Quality control of this data is critical to providing useful information for decision making. Easy retrieval of data from the database(s) is critical to creation of information that can be then evaluated by people or expert systems for identification of trends and comparison of performance in line with target measures.

APPENDIX 4.1 KEY FUNCTIONALITY BY CORE MODULE

Note: This list is not exhaustive, but provides a good guide for someone who is charged with the responsibility to develop CWMS functional requirements.

Asset Records

(1) Support an alphanumeric numbering system for unique identifiers of assets.
(2) Provide an asset classification system by type, subtype and category necessary to easily find the specific asset (e.g., type—mechanical, subtype—pump, category—centrifugal).
(3) Provide a description field (unlimited text).
(4) Provide fields (driven by drop-down lists) for asset criticality and planner or supervisor responsible for the asset.
(5) Provide specification templates (consistent with the asset classifi-

cation system) and unique specifications associated with specific assets.

(6) Provide fields (or tabs) for location and address information for uniquely identifying the asset. These should include x, y and z co-ordinates in the case of linear assets (like sewers and water lines).

(7) Provide fields (or tabs) for original equipment manufacturer (OEM), serial number, date purchased and date installed.

(8) Provide a separate tab for commissioning information unique to the asset (e.g., for a pump: flow, pressure (suction and discharge) vibration, bearing temperature, motor voltage and current).

(9) Allow the setup of preventive maintenance jobs and associated triggering information unique to the asset.

(10) Allow the setup of accounting information necessary to track costs against the asset—general ledger and budget.

(11) Set up bill of materials (BOMs) by asset.

(12) Provide the ability to link and track permits (e.g., hot work, lock/tag out) to the asset.

(13) Provide the ability to link electronic files to the asset (e.g., word documents, drawings, photos, videos).

(14) Allow the setup of additional user-defined fields or tabs for any unique information the user may want to associate with the asset (e.g., the old asset numbers).

(15) Provide the ability to track condition data of the asset based on a numerical scale and the ability to plot the trends graphically.

(16) Provide the ability to track the reliability of the asset based on the following information.

   (a) Mean time between failure (MTBF)

   (b) Mean time to repair (MTRR)

   (c) Average asset uptime (AAU)

(17) Provide the ability to perform editing updates on the asset.

   (a) Make status active, inactive, decommissioned, moth balled

   (b) Copy and delete

Performance Centers

(1) Allow the setup of multiple performance (entity) hierarchies driven by a parent-child relationship.

(2) Provide the ability to graphically show the performance hierarchy.

(3) Provide a classification system for all levels above the asset level to facilitate performance reporting.

(4) Allow text description and other fields necessary to track activities against the performance center (e.g., general ledger codes, budgets, supervisor).

(5) Provide the ability to run reports from any performance center without exiting the entity record.

(6) Provide the ability to do cost reporting (estimated, budgeted, accrued, actuals).

   (a) Roll costs up the hierarchy based on the parent-child relationship.

   (b) Send journal entries to accounts payables by general ledger code.

   (c) Send journal entries to accounts payables by activity code.

(7) Provide budgeting capabilities by performance center.

   (a) Zero-based budgeting

   (b) Based on the previous year's actual cost (increase or decrease by a suitable factor, e.g., inflation)

   (c) Ability to update budgets at any time (usually necessary when there are significant economic changes requiring changes to the budgets)

(8) Provide the ability to link unlimited files to each performance center (as in the case of the asset record).

Work Order Management

Work Order Initiation (Work Requests)

(1) Support the request to do work from the following sources.

   (a) Reactive work
   - emergency work, work necessary to contain a situation threatening the life of asset (not planned)
   - breakdown work, asset fails and all work efforts diverted immediately to getting asset back on line (basic or detailed planning can happen)

   (b) Proactive Work (always planned)
   - preventive work (maintenance)—work triggered by

statistic or calendar-based events aimed at asset preservation (always planned)

- predictive work (maintenance)—specific tasks done at set frequencies to collect data on the condition of the asset
- corrective work (maintenance)—proactive work identified from reactive- or other proactive-type work

(2) Provide the ability to enter a work request type based on the categories identified above.

(3) Provide the ability to identify a description of the requested work and a work priority with each WR.

(4) Provide the ability to link the WR to an asset, GL charge code or activity.

(5) Automatically create WR based on data received from the SCADA system.

(6) Identify duplicate WRs.

(7) Use automatic numbering and electronic date and time stamping of WRs.

(8) Provide the ability to route the completed WR for approval.

(9) Provide the ability to list a symptom code and failure-related data to the WR record.

(10) Provide the ability to reference a defect tag number.

(11) Provide easy-to-use query to locate WRs by type, originator, status, asset, etc.

(12) Provide editing capability for WR records.

(13) Provide the capability to graphically view the WR backlog by WR type asset and originator.

Work Planning (Work Orders)

(1) Support the creation of work orders (WOs) from the following types of WRs.

(a) Reactive work
- emergency work, work necessary to contain a situation threatening the life of asset (not planned)
- breakdown work, asset fails and all work efforts diverted immediately to getting asset back on line (basic or detailed planning can happen)

(b) Proactive work (always planned)
- preventive work (maintenance)—work triggered by

> statistic or calendar-based events aimed at asset preservation (always planned)
> - predictive work (maintenance)—specific tasks done at set frequency to collect data on the condition of the asset
>
>> (c) Corrective work (maintenance)—proactive work identified from reactive- or other proactive-type work

(2) Provide the ability to create a WO from a WR with the problem description as the first task.

(3) Provide the ability to view the work history in order to determine the best approach for carrying out the work on the asset.

(4) Determine if the asset is covered by vendor warranties and should be done by the vendor instead of using internal resources.

(5) Create a detailed job plan with appropriate tasks, supporting documentation and estimated resources requirements (labor, materials, etc.) as follows.
   (a) Manually (build from scratch)
   (b) By copying and editing a previous job plan or standard job
   (c) From an active or previously saved WO

(6) Provide the ability to route the planned WO for approval.

(7) Provide the ability to save the WO as "planning in process".

(8) Provide the ability to the save the WO as a standard job for future use.

(9) Link documents (specifications, instructions, drawings, safety permits, etc.) to the WO record.

(10) Provide the ability to reference a defect tag number on the WO.

(11) Provide easy-to-use query to locate WOs by type, originator, status, asset, etc.

(12) Provide editing capability for WO records.

(13) Provide the capability to view the WO backlog graphically and by WO type asset and originator.

Work Scheduling

(1) Provide the ability to query the active work order backlog by various categories and or system computed weighting based on a combination of work priority, and asset criticality.

(2) Create a daily or weekly schedule by crew, work team, facility, process area or geographic area, as necessary.

(3) Review work orders for scheduling based on availability of resources, tools/equipment, materials/services and availability of the asset to be worked on.

(4) Review schedule compliance from existing (current period) schedules.

(5) Display craft loading and other data relevant to the scheduling function in a graphical format.

(6) Show manpower availability projections by crew.

(7) Assign internal labor resources (individual teams) to WOs.

(8) Assign WOs to schedules and export schedule to project management software to carry out project management-type assignments (start, end dates and dependencies).

(9) Update the CWMS schedule with project management changes.

(10) Forward or print out schedules by teams for planning scheduling meetings.

(11) Provide the ability to make edits to the schedule.

(12) Provide the ability to download schedules to mobile or hand-held devices.

Work Execution/Closeout

(1) Track job progress and charge resources to the overall WO or specific tasks.

(2) Track conformance to safety requirements—permits.

(3) Allow data entry in support of work order closeout—reason for failure, description of work done and resources used.

(4) Allow statistical entry at closeout—asset condition, run hours, baseline predictive data.

(5) Provide time reporting functionality by employee and work order in support of payroll data requirements.

(6) Upload completed work orders from mobile or hand-held devices.

(7) Update documents (associated with the asset worked on) to reflect any changes, e.g., "redlining" of drawings.

(8) Create a follow-up or corrective work order linked to the current work order, based on additional work identified.

Work Evaluation

(1) Have the ability to save relevant cost and work data as history in the work order linked to the asset.

(2) Have the ability to provide easy but detailed queries on work and cost history to evaluate work by asset, performance center or activity code in support of continuous improvement initiatives.

(3) Provide functionality to view asset reliability (mean time between failures).

Preventive Maintenance

(1) Create preventive maintenance jobs complete with task details and supporting resource assignment by asset type.

(2) Link PM jobs to unlimited assets.

(3) Link unlimited PM jobs to individual assets.

(4) Trigger PM jobs based on

    (a) Calendar date

    (b) Run time

    (c) Operating statistic, e.g., fuel consumption

    (d) Condition threshold, e.g., number of holes in a sewer

    (e) Seasonal event, e.g., winterization

    (f) Any combination of the above, whichever comes first

(5) Provide the ability to set up PM routes (e.g., lubrication routes) to make the best use of labor resources.

(6) Provide the ability for automatic triggering of PM.

(7) Provide the ability to do PM forecasting.

(8) Prevent the duplication of PM in the event that PM is not done and the new trigger date comes up again.

(9) Provide editing capability for PM—copy, delete, etc.

(10) Provide query capability to view PM by PM type, asset type, and open PM WOs.

(11) Provide the capability for PM analysis in order to determine the effectiveness of the PM program.

Predictive Maintenance

(1) Provide the ability to collect, track and trend various condition data on assets by predictive technique and/or asset type.

(2) Enable triggering of work requests based on preset thresholds of condition data.

(3) Enable the creation of WOs from these requests with the predictive work type.

(4) Provide the capability for predictive PM and predictive WO analysis in order to determine the effectiveness of the PdM program.

Capital Projects

(1) Create projects with subprojects, tasks and subtasks and unique account codes.

(2) Create various project types in support of asset management.
 (a) New asset creation
 (b) Asset replacement
 (c) Asset modification
 (d) Asset rehabilitation
 (e) Asset decommissioning

(3) Create miscellaneous projects not directly linked to the asset.

(4) Create project budgets and route through the approval process.

(5) Charge resources against the project of activity.

(6) Export project to project management software to carry out project management type assignments (start, end dates and dependencies).

(7) Update the project in the CWMS with project management changes.

(8) Create the asset record (in inactive status) and provide the ability to populate the record with baseline data at time of commissioning.

(9) Provide the ability to query projects by type, account codes, asset etc.

Materials Management

Inventory

(1) Allow for the setup of multiple stock rooms.

(2) Allow for the set up of stock items records and associate them with one or more stock rooms.

(3) Stock item records should contain fields for inventory classifica-

tion, stock item number, description, balance on hand, general ledger code, where used, location data, handling information reorder point (ROP), reorder quantity (ROQ), safety stock level (SSL) and other information consistent with good inventory management practices).

(4) Provide the ability to set up a master catalog for stock and non-stock items.

(5) Provide the ability to link an item to a vendor with associated pricing and availability information (lead time, etc.).

(6) Allow the attachment of relevant documentation to the stock item record, e.g., MSDS sheet.

(7) Perform the following inventory transactions.

    (a) Issues to a WO, project or general ledger code

    (b) Receipts—partial or full

    (c) Returns to stock

    (d) Transfer between stock rooms

    (e) Inventory control—cycle counts and adjustments

(8) Support average, standard, first in first out (FIFO) and last in first out (LIFO) costing methods.

(9) Alert the requisitioner that materials have been received.

(10) Capture statistics necessary for vendor management at the time of receipt.

(11) Provide the ability to track repairable spares.

(12) Provide functionality to set up and manage a tool room.

(13) Support stock item reservations and pick lists necessary for work planning and scheduling.

(14) Support the inventory replenishment process.

    (a) Automatic generation of PRs when the reorder report is run

    (b) Adjustment of ROP and ROQ when the reorder report is evaluated

(15) Provide the ability to identify obsolete, slow moving or surplus stock items.

(16) Support bar coding or stock item transactions and the physical process.

(17) Track and manage inventory carrying costs.

(18) Allow easy inventory queries to locate and access relevant inventory information.

Purchasing

(1) Set up records to support the purchasing process.

    (a) Buyer records—by type of purchase, commodity, stores, dollar limit for purchases

    (b) Vendor ordering—ordering contact information (address, telephone, e-mail), shipping contact information, commodities sold, etc.

    (c) Standard purchasing terms and conditions

    (d) Units of measure

    (e) Exchange rates

    (f) Relevant taxes

(2) Allow for the setup of the purchase requisition (PR) and purchase order (PO) templates.

    (a) Support the purchase of stock, non-stock and services.

    (b) Create manual or automatic PRs (with automatic or manual numbering) in support of the various business processes and route through the approval process.

    (c) Create manual or automatic POs (with automatic or manual numbering) and/or from PRs in support of the various business processes and route through the approval process.

    (d) Allow for the distribution of charges (by percentage) across the entire PR, PO and by line item.

(3) Allow for the setup of purchase item catalog (stock or non-stock relationship with the various vendors).

(4) Support the request for quotation (RFQ) and the contract process (requires the ability to export and import bid information to and from a spreadsheet program for analysis).

(5) Support the blanket order process for just-in-time purchases.

(6) Support credit card process in support of just-in-time purchases.

(7) Provide functionality in support of expediting POs.

(8) Support vendor performance analysis based on data collected in the RFQ, purchasing and receipt processes.

(9) Support extensive queries necessary to manage the requisitioning, purchase order, bidding contracts, and vendor management processes.

(10) Provide standard purchasing management reports.

Workflow

(1) Have central repository for workflow-related actions on sign-on to the CWMS, based on user profiles.
(2) Provide messages based on the user confirming a certain transaction or requesting action.
(3) Enable the approval process for documents (work requests, work orders, budgets, permits, purchase requisitions, purchase orders, invoices, etc.).
   (a) Set up approvers based on dollar limits, document types, or unique functions (e.g., safety or engineering review).
   (b) Set up substitute approvers (based on start and end dates).
   (c) Support electronic signatures with appropriate security.
(4) Track and recognize the need for action based on warranty and guarantee for goods and services purchased.
(5) Allow seamless integration to productivity tools necessary to support the work, asset and materials management processes (e.g., e-mail, project scheduling software).
(6) Provide the flexibility to configure workflow actions based on unique needs.

Performance Management

(1) Provide the ability for the user to create algorithms using specific CWMS information to compute information
   (a) necessary to support the work process—e.g., PM and schedule compliance, asset reliability, manpower effectiveness.
   (b) necessary to support the asset management process.
   (c) necessary to support the operations process.
(2) Provide the ability to view performance scorecards by performance center.
(3) Provide the ability to trend performance metrics and present graphically.

CHAPTER 5

CWMS Support Modules and Features

Over the past years there has been a trend by CWMS vendors to develop additional functionality (in addition to the core work order, inventory and purchasing modules) to meet the needs of clients for a stopgap solution. It is therefore not uncommon to find CWMS solutions offering modules in the areas of accounts payables, accounts receivables, document management, permitting, fleet management, reliability engineering, performance management and report writing (Figure 5.1).

Usually these modules are included in the price of the software whether you need them or not. They are usually switched off if not needed (e.g., you may have another accounts payables or document management solution) or they are used in a manner transparent to the user to support interfaces to existing systems. This concept is discussed in more detail in Chapter 6. The following discussions review the key features of these modules necessary to support the work management process.

BUDGETING AND GENERAL LEDGER

Everything comes down to dollars—at least from the accounting perspective. Generally, the budget and expenditure process has to be tracked against the work management process to ensure that funds are used as planned, during the timeframe projected, and are charged to the right buckets for tracking. It is therefore important that the CWMS carry a complete set of general ledger (GL) account codes necessary to support the work and capital project processes. There should be functionality that allows budgeting at various performance center levels (with an associ-

73

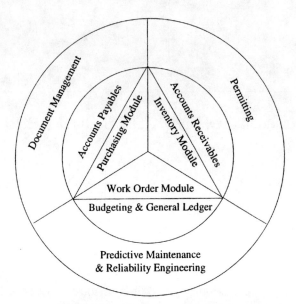

FIGURE 5.1 *CWMS Support Modules.*

ated GL code) and the ability to track all expenditures at any point in time in the categories of estimated, committed and actuals. An approval process ensures the flexibility of empowerment and trusting of employees or control necessary to manage expenditures. Expenditures can arise from:

- purchase of materials and services
- purchase of new equipment
- purchase of rental equipment
- inventory transactions (issues, returns, receipts, write-offs)
- labor costs (regular and overtime)

Journal entries (JEs) are generated for each of these transactions and need to be fed to the financial system on a regular basis to support the budget control, payment, payroll and cash management processes. Similarly, any changes in GL codes and budget figures should be fed on a regular basis to the CWMS AP module to ensure that costs are properly managed with budgets and charged to the appropriate GL codes.

FINANCIALS—ACCOUNTS PAYABLES AND INVOICING

The invoicing function is another highly desirable functionality in the

CWMS to support the accounts payables process. The key requirement here is the need to support the three-way matching process (Figure 5.2).

This is a standard process in most organizations and provides the much needed confidence that invoices for payments exactly match the purchase order items with the goods and services received. This process should be automatic at vendor invoice entry stage, allowing internal comparison of receipt information with purchase order information and invoice information. All exceptions are automatically routed to the appropriate person for resolution, these could be the following.

- PO and invoice information does not match receipt (in this case the warehouse supervisor needs to address this issue).
- Invoice information does not match PO and receipt (the vendor then needs to correct this).
- Receipt and invoice information do not match the PO (the buyer must then resolve this situation).
- A worst case situation is that none of the three types of information match (vendor, buyer, invoice clerk and warehouse supervisor must then all participate in resolving the problem).

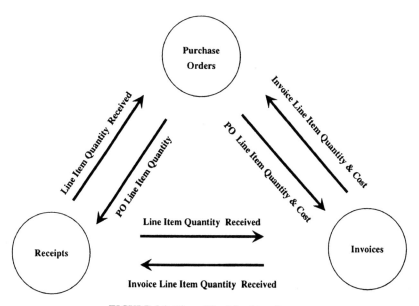

FIGURE 5.2 Three-Way Matching Process.

ACCOUNTS RECEIVABLES

This is a need that is widely used in most businesses to account for revenue from sale of products or services (this functionality generally resides in the financials system). However, the CWMS should be able to identify work orders that are being done for outside parties. This would be applicable to a machine shop or laboratory-type operations. In this case there would be a need to identify the cost of the service so that an appropriate invoice can be created to the customer using the financial system.

DOCUMENT MANAGEMENT

The work management process depends on much key documentation linked to an asset, a stock item or a vendor. These can be specifications, procedures, safety and permitting instructions, material safety data sheets (MSDS), drawings, photographs or investigative reports. Many CWMS provide the ability to store this information within the CWMS database and allow the user to access it during the work management process. This approach provides only simple document management functionality and basic features such as security, version control and records management are not usually provided. The trend is to manage documents in a proper electronic document management system (EDMS) with appropriate links to the necessary asset, vendor and stock records.

PERMITTING MODULE

Permitting is a critical business requirement in the work management process. It is extremely important that all work is carried out in a safe and environmentally sound manner. In this regard, hot work, confined space entry, lock and tag out, safe work, excavation, hazardous energy and others must be generated at the appropriate point in the work management process. The system should be able to link the permits with the work order, identify qualified employees (based on training records) and reference the relevant procedures (possibly in an EDMS). Permit closeout must be integral to the work order closeout process.

VEHICLE OR FLEET MANAGEMENT

Some CWMS systems provide specific functionality in support of vehicle maintenance, addressing special requirements such as leases, warranty-type repairs, license and insurance renewal, triggering of PM based on fuel consumption, rental charge and depreciation. This is important for effective fleet management around the vehicle life cycle. Recently, many CWMS vendors have been able to accommodate these special business requirements in the normal work order functionality through use of user-defined fields in the asset setup and unique business rules. Innovative configuration ideas have allowed many CWMS users to support the work process around their fleet operations using the same CWMS that is used for its other assets. In this case a vehicle is considered to be an asset just like any other asset in the operations.

RELIABILITY ENGINEERING

Many businesses that have embarked on work improvement strategies with enabling CWMS systems are seriously considering (some are employing) optimized work concepts. Here the focus is on moving from doing assigned tasks efficiently to effectiveness—doing the right tasks efficiently. It is very important in asset preservation that the right work tactics are identified and are incorporated into the overall work program for the asset. The CWMS should also allow tracking of reliability-type performance metrics such as mean time between failures (MTBF) and mean time to repair (MTTR).

REPORT WRITER

When a CWMS is implemented, there are usually a lot of records (user, asset, stock items, documents, PM) set up before any people start using the system. During the course of doing work, these records are continually updated and new data is created (WRs, WOs, PRs, POs, stock transactions). It is obvious that there has to be a simple way of making sense of the data in this database. This data must be grouped into data subsets to create information based on the user's unique business needs. This information combined with the user's experience, skills and expertise create the knowledge vital for day-to-day decision making, performance management and continuous improvement.

APPENDIX 5.1 KEY FUNCTIONALITY BY SUPPORT MODULE

Note: This list is not exhaustive, but provides a good guide for someone who is charged with the responsibility to develop CWMS functional requirements.

Invoicing

(1) Support various types of invoices—purchase order, advance payments to POs, recurrent (e.g., rental payments), freight charges, credit card purchases.

(2) Provide support for three-way matching of invoices.

    (a) Purchase order line item quantity and price

    (b) Receipt line item quantity and price

    (c) Invoice line item quantity and price

    (d) Exception reporting with reports routed to the buyer, stores keeper or vendor for rectification

(3) Support the following requirements in the invoicing process.

    (a) Accrue taxes by invoice line item.

    (b) Take advantage of vendor discounts.

    (c) Set up user-defined tolerances.

(4) Provide drill down to stores and purchase order records from the invoicing to resolve invoicing exceptions.

(5) Provide an electronic file of approved invoices for payment to the accounts payables module of the financial system.

Budgeting and General Ledger

(1) Provide the ability to conduct zero-based budgeting in support of the work management process.

(2) Set up budgets by performance center, asset and activity based costing code.

(3) Provide the ability to check for funds availability against budgets before any funds are committed in the work, operations, asset and materials management processes.

(4) Support the budget approval process and routing through predefined electronic approval routes.

(5) Set up unlimited general ledger codes to support the work, asset, operations and materials management process (could be populated from the financial module) to track costs as follows.

    (a) Budget

    (b) Estimated

    (c) Committed or accrued

    (d) Actual

Accounts Receivables

This is not intended to provide the full requirements for accounts receivables (AR), but rather to highlight AR as it applies to the work management process.

(1) Track cost of work, goods and services that should be charged to other groups, e.g., work done by the machine shop, building services, studies done by engineering etc.
(2) Create internal invoices for any charges in (1) above and send to the invoicing module for processing.

Document Management

This is not intended to provide the full requirements for document management, but rather to highlight documents management requirements necessary to support the work management process.

(1) Provide the ability to create a user-defined profile as follows.
    (a) Unique document number and version
    (b) Document name and brief description of contents
    (c) Associated asset, performance center, project, etc.
    (d) Date and time stamp for each change in the document
    (e) Location of file
(2) Support the following document types.
    (a) Word documents
    (b) Drawings
    (c) Spreadsheets
    (d) Small databases, e.g., Microsoft Access files
    (e) Process charts
    (f) Presentations
    (g) Pictures
    (h) Videos
(3) Support the following document transactions.
    (a) Add a new document as per display profile and set up security access.
    (b) Update an existing document.
    (c) View an existing document.
    (d) Check out a copy of a document to an approved user.

(4) Provide security for documents.
  (a) Set up approved users.
  (b) Provide the ability to limit read-only and edit capabilities of documents' specified users.
  (c) Provide a history trail of all changes and access for documents.
  (d) Track and notify the system administrator of all unauthorized access of documents or attempts to do so.
(5) Provide the ability to archive documents based on user-specified parameters.
(6) Provide query and search capability to allow users to easily find documents in support of the various business processes.

Permitting (Safety)

(1) Provide support for regulatory compliance for material safety data sheets (MSDS)—manage status, revisions, etc.
(2) Allow the creation of various work-related permit types.
  (a) Hot work
  (b) Lock and tag out
  (c) Excavation
  (d) Elevated work
  (e) Confined space entry
  (f) Hazardous materials handling
(3) Provide the ability to identify and assign qualified resources specific to the permit type.
(4) Provide the ability to link documents to a permit.
(5) Provide the ability to link a permit to a specific work order or group of work orders.
(6) Allow for tracking of the permit over its life—creation to closure.
(7) Allow for capture of permit-related data at time of work execution as needed to support regulations.
(8) Allow for queries on various permit types—open and closed.

Report Writer

The CWMS should provide a standard report writer (or seamlessly integrate to one) allowing the following functionalities.

(1) Allow user friendly access to data in the various databases.

(2) Allow simple development of user-defined graphic- or text-based reports (based on the data residing in the various databases).

(3) Create advanced reports in the support of performance management, allowing for simple algorithms and computations.

(4) Provide the ability to save this report as unique to the user or make into a standard report accessible to the wider user community.

(5) Provide standard reports (graphic- as well as text-based) from the vendor as per the following examples.

    (a) WR backlog

    (b) WO backlog

    (c) PM listing by category

    (d) PM and schedule compliance

    (e) Asset cost by asset category and cost type

    (f) Reason for failure by asset type

    (g) Open orders list by vendor

    (h) Vendor performance by vendor

    (i) Slow moving stock items

    (j) Inventory ABC analysis

    (k) Receiving report

    (l) Physical adjustment report

    (m) Approved invoices for payments

    (n) Inventory value

    (o) Inventory turns

CHAPTER 6

Integration into a Complete Computerized Business Tool

INTRODUCTION

Integration of the CWMS modules into other technology solutions is fast becoming a necessity in most operations today. The need for an integrated solution is discussed in this chapter. The concept of the system development life cycle (SDLC) (Figure 6.1) is developed as a means to effectively manage an integrated technology solution. All possible interfaces to other applications are listed and the requirements are defined. In particular, the interfaces to a financial system are discussed in detail because of the critical importance of this link. The chapter is then rounded off with a discussion on the various techniques and methodologies that are used in integration and interface development today.

WHY AN INTEGRATED TECHNOLOGY SOLUTION?

A good strategic plan identifies corporate objectives and performance targets in line with the business that the company is in. These objectives and performance targets are disaggregated to the business units and from them down to the last team in the field or on the shop floor. These objectives cannot be achieved in isolation or they must meet the desired performance targets required by business units, departments, divisions and teams to work together. Each unique area would use enabling business applications to support their work practices (e.g., financial, human resources, geographical information, customer billing, process control, scada systems). It is obvious that the corporation cannot rely on verbal or

83

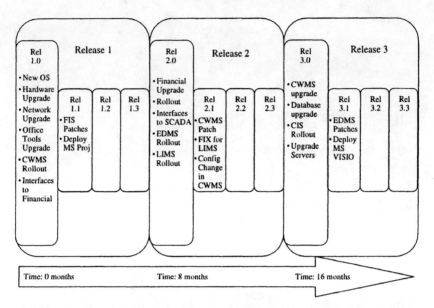

FIGURE 6.1 *System Development Methodology for an Integrated Technology Solution—The System Development Life Cycle (SDLC).*

paper-based methods to provide transactions or information on a timely basis to other groups. In reality, a number of companies actually do just that with consequential inefficiencies. The ideal solution is the concept of integrated technology that is designed to support work processes of all units which focus on the performance management framework. A typical integrated technology solution is seen in Figure 6.2.

INTEGRATION METHODOLOGIES

System integration can start at the business application level. Here it is possible to trade off functionality for interface complexity in arriving at a manageable integrated solution. Obviously, if a lot of core functionality can be identified in a CWMS then there will be a reduced need for interfaces. On one extreme, a best of breed approach can be adopted where the best type of business application can be selected and appropriate interfaces developed. This can clearly lead to a very complex solution. Conversely, one can seek one business application that provides all the desired functionality of an integrated technology solution. In reality, a point somewhere along this continuum is usually selected which is driven by existing business systems that are impractical or too costly to change. Sometimes, you may have to live with a certain level of duplication: for example, two purchasing modules (one in a CWMS and the other in the financial system). In this example, it is too difficult to switch off the CWMS purchasing functions and build all the necessary interfaces to the financial system. When both modules are used, interfaces can be limited to PRs and receiving information to the financial system, POs and vendor updates to the CWMS. The complexity of the interfaces may depend on the type of data that has to be transferred and the timing of the actual transfer. There are three design parameters in this case: real time (where changes in one system are instantaneously reflected in the other), near real time (changes reflected after a few seconds delay) and batch (where changes are reflected after a longer designated time interval, e.g., daily, weekly or monthly). Batch data transfer can be done either manually or automatically.

Actual interface development can be designed based on "hard" interfaces directly to the respective business applications or through an intermediary system called "middleware" that acts as a data transfer agent. In the first instance, any changes in the business systems that affect data transfer would require revisiting and updating all interfaces to that sys-

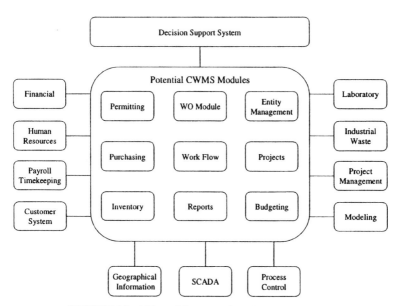

FIGURE 6.2 *A Typical Integrated Technology Solution.*

TABLE 6.1.

Business Practice Area	Data Set	From Business Application	To Business Application	Timing and Frequency
Work Management Process	Changes to the GL	FIS	CWMS	Batch
	Budget $ by GL code	FIS	CWMS	Real time
	Actual $ (paid in FIS)	FIS	CWMS	Batch
	Estimated $ by GL code	CWMS	FIS	Real time
	Accrual $ by GL code	CWMS	FIS	Real time
	Approved invoice journal entries for payment	CWMS	FIS	Batch
	Labor $ to payroll	CWMS	FIS	Batch
	Employee qualifications	HRMS	CWMS	Batch
	Employee record changes (position, salary etc.)	HRMS	CWMS	Batch
	Customer service requests	GIS, CIS	CWMS	Real time
	Active WR and WOs	CWMS	GIS, CIS	Batch
	WO backlog count	DSS	CWMS	Batch
	PM compliance	DSS	CWMS	Batch
	Asset-related documents	EDMS	CWMS	Real time
	Updates to asset-related documents from the work order process	CWMS	EDMS	Real time
Operations Management	Condition data on assets	CBMS, SCADA	CWMS, GIS	Near real time
	Asset operational data - e.g. flow, pressure	SCADA	CWMS, DSS	Near real time
	Asset fault and alarm conditions	SCADA	CWMS	Real Time
	Chemical and electricity usage	SCADA	DSS, CWMS	Batch
Materials Management Process	Budget $ by GL code	FIS	CWMS	Real time
	Changes to $ on the inventory GL based on materials management transactions	CWMS	FIS	Batch

(continued)

TABLE 6.1 (continued).

Business Practice Area	Data Set	From Business Application	To Business Application	Timing and Frequency
Materials Management Process (continued)	Encumbrances (committals) for purchase orders or blanket orders	CWMS	FIS	Batch
	Receipt Information needed to support the invoicing process	CWMS	FIS	Batch
	Exceptions from the three-way matching process in accounts payables	FIS	CWMS	Batch
	Changes to the vendor record	FIS	CWMS	Real time
	Vendor performance information	CWMS	FIS	Batch
Asset Management Process	Update to the asset record (location information)	GIS	CWMS, AMS	Real Time
	Condition data (e.g. repairs on water or sewer lines)	CWMS, CBMS	GIS, AMS	Real Time
	Projected deterioration curves	AMS	CWMS, DSS	Batch
	Internal labor costs for capital projects	CWMS	FIS	Batch
	Capital improvement projects from modeling exercises in the AMS	AMS	CWMS	Batch
	GASB 34 reporting data requirements	CWMS, AMS, FIS	DSS	Batch
	CMOM data reporting requirements	CWMS, AMS, FIS	DSS	Batch

Typical business applications:
DSS - decision support system
CWMS - computerized work management system
FIS - financial system
HRMS - human resources management system
SCADA - supervisory control and data acquisition system
GIS - geographical information system
EDMS - electronic documents management system
AMS - asset management system
ERP - enterprise resource planning system
CIS - customer information system
CBMS - condition monitoring systems

tem (this can prove to be a costly effort). In the latter approach, only the interface to the system and the middleware needs to be updated. This approach provides much more flexibility in managing the integrated technology solution as well as an overall lower system development and maintenance cost.

DATA TRANSFER REQUIREMENTS FOR AN INTEGRATED TECHNOLOGY SOLUTION

Table 6.1 lists the typical data transfer requirements to and from the major business applications needed to support business processes:

CONFIGURATION MANAGEMENT NECESSARY FOR AN INTEGRATED TECHNOLOGY SOLUTION

When an integrated view of technology is considered for the support of work practices it is very important that adequate attention is given to managing changes in the various components that make up the integrated solution. There may be changes driven by specific users that would have impacts on users at various levels (e.g., the addition of another WR type will be seen by everyone in the system—(many of these users may not need it). Similarly, there may be changes driven by error corrections, new releases from the vendor for specific products or changes in operating system or databases. It is necessary to implement a change request process that properly identifies the desired change, the potential benefits, the impacted users and business systems, the level of urgency (priority) and a supporting business case. Such change requests should be channeled to a working committee (with representatives from various disciplines—information technology, system administrators and divisional business representatives). This group should review these requests, be in line with the SDLC framework and provide guidance for a coordinated approach to implementation in the form of subreleases (e.g., Rel 1.1) or new releases (e.g., Rel 2.0) of the integrated solution.

CHAPTER 7

Hardware and Operating Environment

INTRODUCTION

Users of a CWMS work at a terminal and use printers to produce work requests, work orders, inventory pick lists, purchase requisitions, purchase orders and necessary reports. The system can run on a stand-alone personal computer (microcomputer), a networked minicomputer system, a mainframe computer or a client server system. All of the above systems permit placing terminals on the desks of personnel who need to create work-related records, retrieve stored records, review history and prepare daily reports needed in the work management process. In the simplest form, it is possible to load and operate the CWMS software on one personal computer. This option is clearly limiting, both in terms of accessibility by the various personnel (who need to use the systems on a routine basis to carry out work) as well as storage space for data. We will focus our discussion on the mainframe, minicomputer and client server hardware systems because they are more likely to be applicable to most situations. Appendix 7.1 provides a template for developing the technology requirement for a CWMS project.

MAINFRAME AND MINICOMPUTER INFRASTRUCTURE

The mainframe and minicomputer system are some of the earliest types of computer hardware that were developed (Figure 7.1). These systems date back at least 10 to 20 years ago. Many system manufacturers

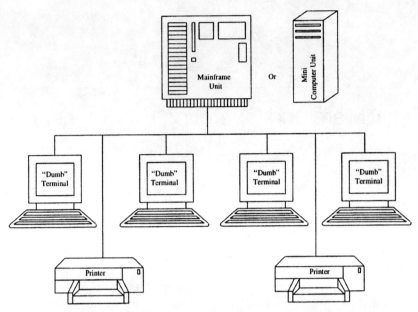

FIGURE 7.1 *Mainframe/Minicomputer Hardware Configuration.*

still support this type of technology, providing new models and or replacement parts. In the past, elaborate programs were written in various languages (e.g., COBOL) to support many business functions. The program and data resides on the minicomputer, the display and data entry are done on the terminals. (Note that a minicomputer is a small version of a mainframe; it has about the same rating characteristics but is considerably less powerful and less expensive.) Many companies still operate mainframe and minicomputer systems and run "homegrown" systems on these hardware platforms. This presents a major hurdle when they consider selection and implementation of current CWMS applications because of compatibility issues and tremendous costs in interface development. The current trend in hardware platforms is to move away from the mainframe and minicomputer systems and take advantage of the cheaper, more flexible and easier to manage client server systems.

CLIENT SERVER [WIDE AREA NETWORK (WAN) AND LOCAL AREA NETWORK (LAN)]

The stand-alone personal computer unit is one in which the CWMS program and data are stored on the unit and it is used to carry out the work process. A networked minicomputer system is generally a group of terminals connected to a powerful minicomputer. A client server system is a network of personal computers, called clients or workstations, connected to powerful computers called servers (Figure 7.2). This is the most popular type of system used to operate CWMS today. The clients can store data, programs and perform operations or can access data and programs from the servers. The continued rapid advances in computer hardware technology in the area of central processing unit (CPU) speed (from less than 75 MHz 10 years ago to over 2 GHz today), storage capacity (from less than 256 kilobytes 10 years ago to over 100 gigabytes today) and networking connectivity have vastly increased the volume of data that can be transferred in real time. In addition, it is now possible to deploy the business applications (e.g., CWMS) and the databases on separate servers to improve performance and system reliability. Recent advances in system maintenance software allow remote deployment and mainte-

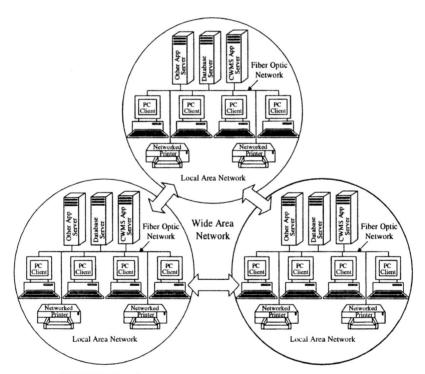

FIGURE 7.2 *Client Server Configuration (Including WAN/LAN).*

nance of the software through the use of system administration business tools.

When you are considering the implementation of a CWMS there are number of hardware requirements that need to be addressed and they should be specified in the request for information and request for proposal. Here is a suggested list for consideration.

(1) Number of current users (determines the number of computer clients to be deployed)

(2) "Fat" or "thin" clients—"fat" refers to the practice of installing a copy of the CWMS application on the client computer, making it very easy to access the software and database when needed to support the work management process. In the event that the main servers go down, a user can still access the CWMS through his computer. Improved server reliability and accessibility from a central server has now made it possible to effectively run a "thin" client configuration where both the application and the database reside elsewhere (on application and database servers). In the latter case, it is easier for the system administrator to make upgrades or changes to the system without having to access every client out in the field. This is the most popular configuration used by companies today.

(3) Network connectivity is a key area to be addressed. This refers to the method of connecting the various hardware components. There are two types of networks: the local area network (LAN) and the wide area network (WAN). The LAN is the local networked servers and client computers usually connected by hard wiring (Ethernet or fiber optic cables)—system performance is usually very good (fast response times). The WAN is the connection of all the LANs to form a connected system providing wider access to users. The system can also be connected by hard wiring if fiber optic backbones are available (from the local telephone or cable company) and by remote connections (telephone lines, wireless or satellite signals). WANs can sometimes become bogged down by limitations in the capacity of the network infrastructure. However, this is slowly becoming a nonissue with the advances in fiber optics and wireless technology.

(4) Total storage space for the CWMS application program (can be easily specified by the vendor)

(5) Total storage space for CWMS database—the various CWMS-related records that will be created and stored (Note that some of

these records will generally be created prior to the system startup, changing only when the new data is added and some will be created in the course of doing work.)

  (a) User records

  (b) Asset records (including specifications, procedures etc.)

  (c) Documents—drawings, permit procedures

  (d) Work request (WR)

  (e) Work orders (WO)

  (f) Preventive maintenance (PM)

  (g) Permits

  (h) Stock item records

  (i) Stock item vendor records

  (j) Warehouse

  (k) Material safety data sheets (MSDS)

  (l) Stock transaction records

  m. Vendor records

  (n) Purchase requisitions (PR)

  (o) Purchase orders (PO)

  (p) Request for quotations (RFQ)

  (q) Contract records

  (r) General ledger accounting records

  (s) Number of concurrent users

  (t) Estimated number of transactions per hour

  (u) Peak number of transactions

It is important to note that identifying archiving (records saved to disk or tape and are no longer accessible to the CMWS) requirements (e.g., POs to be kept for only seven years) can significantly impact storage requirements. Archiving will be determined by federal regulations for records management as well as internal company policy.

(6) Client location could also be a key consideration especially if some computers will be sited in industrial-type conditions (e.g., workshops, process plants etc.), this may dictate the need for ruggedized-type units.

(7) Other hardware considerations would be necessary if there is a need for mobile computing devices to support work management. This will be discussed in detail in the following section.

MOBILE COMPUTING

Fixed client PCs in carefully specified locations usually satisfy the needs of personnel involved in the work management process. This is the case when personnel work in close proximity to the computer (e.g., in a building). However, many crews traverse large geographic areas during the course of doing work (e.g., pipeline repair crews, water distribution system operators) and they need access to the CWMS during the day. It is therefore important that they can access the CWMS through a laptop computer, personal digital assistant (PDA) or pen-tablet. In the case of the laptop, there can be communications to the system real time through telephone lines or microwave transmission. The PDA and pen-tablet devices are usually used to download data prior to going out in the field, capture the day's work on the device (e.g., PM information) and upload it to the computer when the worker is back in the office at the end of the day. This technology is in its infancy as it applies to the CWMS due to limitations in the storage capacity of the PDA and pen-tablet devices; and in the case of the laptop, limitations in bandwidth and the amount of data that can be transmitted through the wireless modem.

OPERATING PLATFORM

Many CWMS vendors design their software to operate on various operating platforms, e.g., UNIX and Windows NT. It becomes more complicated and costly when the vendor tries to design their CWMS to run on many systems; vendors tend to stick with some of the more common systems available. This means that they keep in touch with the vendors of these operating systems and try to stay in step with their upgrades and new releases. Sometimes this drives the release process for the CWMS vendor's software. Similarly, a company would have standardized on operating system for their hardware-software combination. This means they will have access to a limited number of vendors whose software runs on the same operating system. Unless plans are made to change out an operating system, it is extremely important that the desired operating system is specified in the request for information (RFI) and request for proposal (RFP).

DATABASE CONSIDERATIONS

The database is the next big decision faced when making a decision on a CWMS. In the past, the CWMS vendor included a minidatabase as part of the software but found that it was a costly approach and limited system marketability as a result. Today, the CWMS comes as an application minus the database—the vendor expects that the company will provide the database (this can be SYBASE, ORACLE etc.). The CWMS application will provide all the functionality for conducting the work management process by accessing the database for various records (user, assets, PM, history, WOs) and creating new records in the course of doing work that are then stored in the database. As in the case of operating systems discussed above, vendors design their products to work on certain databases—thus, limiting the choices. Therefore, it is important that database requirements are cleared in the RFI/RFP. There is also a need to cater for additional database user licenses to match the planned number of CWMS users.

THE CWMS AND THE INTERNET

Like almost everything else in life, the Internet has also impacted the future of the CWMS industry. Many vendors have already tapped into the power of the Internet and have developed and deployed first-generation web-based CWMS products. Essentially, in these systems, system access is through the company's intranet through web pages. This allows for easy accessibility where both a WAN and a LAN are in use. The idea of application service providers (ASPs) is being explored by many software vendors as well as entrepreneurial firms. Here, the vendor or firm owns the servers and applications and charge a fee for using the application to conduct business (via the Internet). All data (see list above) is stored on the server at the vendor's site or server farm. This provides a CWMS solution where there is no worry about CWMS software application and database maintenance and upgrade. All of this happens behind the scenes, transparent to the end user. Although this seems to be a very attractive idea it has not caught on so far, possibly due to the reluctance of companies to give over control of all the data that supports their business to a third party.

APPENDIX 7.1 TEMPLATE FOR DEVELOPING THE TECHNOLOGY REQUIREMENTS FOR A CWMS PROJECT

Application Architecture

(1) Support the deployment of a web-based system, allowing access of the system from a standard internet browser.

(2) Provide an open architecture suitable for integrating with other systems.

(3) Have the scalability to support a large number of concurrent users.

(4) Provide support for use of MS Office productivity tools using dynamic data exchange (DDE), object linking and embedding (OLE), e-mail messaging (SMTP and MAPI), etc.

(5) Support communications standard, e.g., TCP/IP network communications protocols.

Operating System Requirements

(1) Indicate what operating system is being used (or will be used) in your technology environment.

(a) Servers

(b) Client computers

(c) Mobile devices

Application and User Security (for Control and Access to the CWMS)

(1) Allow the system administrator to monitor and control access to the various functions of the CWMS.

(2) Provide system access through assigned user profiles and passwords.

(3) Limit user access with modules, queries and reports.

(4) Provide an audit trail that captures user-related information (date, time, etc.) when changes are posted to the database.

Desktop Computers

(1) Provide your requirements on CPU speed, data storage, system memory, operating system and drives. An example is given below.

- desktop computers—Pentium IV, 2.0 GHz, 80 Gig Hard Drive, 512 MB SDRAM and 2GB RDRAM memory, Microsoft XP operating system, CDW 40x60
- laptop computers—Pentium IV, 2.0 GHz, 80 Gig Hard Drive, 512 MB SDRAM and 2GB RDRAM memory, Microsoft XP operating system, CDW 40x60

(2) Provide similar requirements for your servers and disk storage, mobile devices, printers and other peripheral devices.

Network Connectivity

(1) Describe your current local area network (LAN) and wide area network (WAN) specifications and any plans to upgrade in the future.
(2) Describe any special communications requirements (e.g., wireless, microwave) needed to support mobile devices or communications from remote locations.

General note: provide system drawings and access to your IT strategic plan, if possible. This allows the vendor proposing on your project to be better able to determine the compatibility of their product with your current and proposed technology environment.

CHAPTER 8

Selecting and Acquiring the Most Appropriate CWMS for Operations

THE CWMS JUNGLE OUT THERE

Globalization has been a driving force for companies to manufacture products or provide services more cost effectively in order to compete and survive. As a result, companies have re-engineered themselves making the production department very lean. They have also introduced much more complex and automated equipment whose maintenance requirements were much higher. The maintenance department was generally regarded as a necessary evil and this area was not generally targeted for re-engineering. Today, with the unrelenting pressure from competing industries, companies are slowly realizing that there is a wealth of savings to be made using a successfully implemented CWMS to execute a strategic maintenance management strategy and manage all work in a cost-effective manner. As a result, there has been a boom in the CWMS industry with a number of companies (>250) selling hundreds of CWMS products and related services. This boom is projected to continue well into the twenty-first century. As CWMS software vendors try to get the edge on the competition, some have developed specialized products for certain industries (e.g., electric, mining, fleet), some have targeted small businesses, middle-size businesses and large corporations. Selecting the right vendor and software application for the right business is obviously a daunting task.

USING CONSULTING HELP OR DOING IT YOURSELF—THE A TO Z CONCEPT

Many companies have tried to select and implement a CWMS internally and have not been successful, in part, because of lack of experience, lack of resources and a lack of sponsorship within the organization for the project. Conversely, many companies have spent untold fortunes on consulting fees to select and implement a CWMS and have many horror stories to tell about the experience. Figure 8.1 depicts the "A to Z selection concept." Essentially, selection (as well as implementation) can be viewed as a continuum: at one end of the spectrum, a consultant is hired to do everything on behalf of the client with minimal involvement by client employees; At the other end, the client undertakes the entire project in-house with very little external (consulting and vendor) support. Both approaches are fraught with problems. In the first example, using external resources can result in a quick selection process and incorporation of best in class practices but is usually very costly, allows for very little knowledge transfer to in-house staff and poor system acceptance by users. In the second example, there can be a low-cost project with a high level of buy-in and ownership but this usually takes a very long time and the existing work processes are generally duplicated. This means that when a company is doing poor work management using a paper-based process, after implementing the CWMS, they are then doing poor work management using a computer and software! The obvious solution is a mix of external and internal resources to create a cost-effective solution that incorporates best in class work processes, maximizes knowledge transfer (shown in Figure 8.2) to internal staff and maximizes system acceptance and usage. The different steps in the selection process are shown in Figure 8.3.

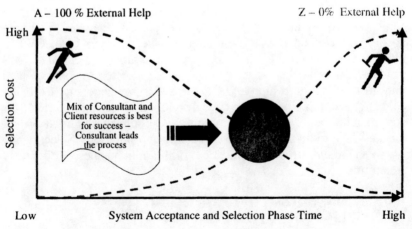

FIGURE 8.1 *The A to Z Selection and Implementation Concept.*

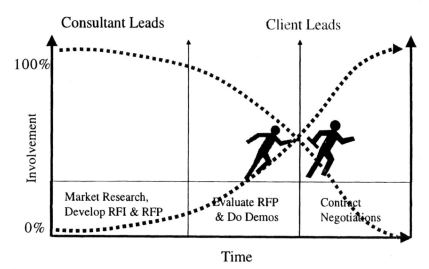

FIGURE 8.2 *Selection Process Maximizes Knowledge Transfer.*

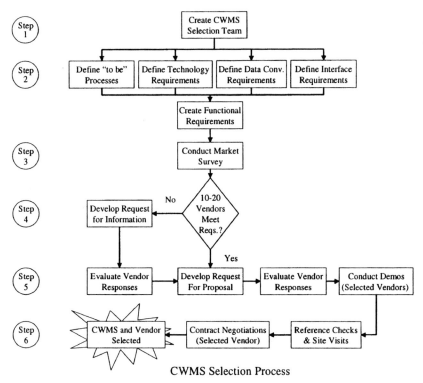

FIGURE 8.3 *The Six-Step CWMS Selection Process.*

Step 1—Planning Phase: Select Internal Team Members, Consultant and Project Kick-off

The first step in the process, after the need for CWMS and its justification is completed, is to acquire the right consulting resources to partner with you in your CWMS project. It would be advisable to consider retaining this resource for the entire selection and implementation phases of the project. This means defining the scope of the services required, developing a request for proposal for consulting services and selecting a suitable candidate. Sometimes it is possible to select a consultant without having to go through a competitive process if it can be shown that the candidate is uniquely qualified and has good references. Once the consultant is engaged, the first responsibility is to work with the CWMS project sponsor to determine the best internal team members to form part of the selection team. This group must have the all the skill sets necessary to successfully select a consultant to partner on the project as well as be able to understand all aspects of the current business processes (work, operations, materials and asset management). In addition, knowledge of the company's general ledger, accounts payables and budgeting systems would be necessary for developing the functional requirements (a later step in the selection process). The start of the CMWS selection phase is a major opportunity for buy-in to the idea of using a CWMS to support work management and, as such, selection of team members is a very important step in the process. Similarly, establishing the right internal leadership for the CWMS project at this stage is very critical to success. The desired qualifications, experience, roles and responsibilities of the team leader are given in Appendix 8.1. The following are the typical resources that can make up the selection team: maintenance tradesperson (mechanic or electrician), operator, materials manager, maintenance engineer, accounts payables clerk, systems analyst (IT), customer service clerk. A complete list of desired roles and responsibilities together with qualifications and experience is given in Appendix 8.1.

Once the team is established, team members are then provided with background information on the project (business case, expected results and high-level project plan). High-level orientation on the selection and implementation process as well as best practice concepts applicable to work, asset, operations and materials management would then be a great way to provide the basic orientation to the team. The team can now complete the planning process by developing a project plan for the selection phase and the detailed communication plan for the project, ensuring the identification of the right message, the intended audience, the communication medium, the frequency of communication and the feedback mechanism. A sample project plan is given in Appendix 8.2 and a sample communication plan is provided in Appendix 8.3.

Step 2—The Market Survey

The market survey is the first step in the process to help make sense out of the 250+ systems in the market. It is also a step that can be done instead of the RFI (step 3) if there is an experienced consultant helping in the selection process. It is first necessary to understand the high-level functionality needed to support business needs, general system size (number of users, expected data requirements), desired database, operating system and some criteria around the desired CWMS vendor with whom you would like to partner. Based on this information, it is usually possible to identify at least 10 to 20 vendors who might be able to meet your CWMS requirements. The sources of information about these companies can be from the consultant's database of vendors, the Internet and various other software information sources. If a market survey is conducted instead of an RFI, it is possible to reduce the selection time by at least six to eight weeks.

Step 3—The Request for Information (RFI) and the Scoring Process

In the event that the market survey is not considered (based on fears of litigation from vendors, who may think they were not given a fair chance to bid) or the survey does not produce an adequate list of vendors then the RFI process must be followed. Essentially, the RFI goes out to all vendors through print media and on your company website in an effort to attract as much interest as possible. In addition, your consultant should have a feel for the vendors and products that would match your needs and should be able to develop a list of 10 to 15 vendors to which the RFI should be sent. It is important that these vendors see your RFI. Careful specifications would ensure that only vendors who really think they are a match for your requirements would respond. The objective at this stage is to identify at least ten vendors who should move on to the RFP phase of the selection process. A sample RFI and RFI scoring spreadsheet is given in Appendix 8.4 and 8.5, respectively. RFI's responses should be evaluated and scored based on the following criteria.

- vendor
  —sound financial standing (Dunn and Bradstreet report if possi-

ble)—if the company (vendor) trades publicly then last three years' financial statements should be reviewed
—vision and mission statement
—investment in product research and development reflected by regular product releases
—at least three reference sites similar to your business
—active user group
—user friendly (and very informative) website company
- product
  —meet or exceed major functional requirements
  —provides additional software modules as part of the core product
  —clearly identifies any third-party software needed to make the product work
  —compatible with desired technology needs
  —ability to provide timely offsite and onsite support
  —provides desirable software licensing options
  —product demos are user friendly and show how the key modules work together

Step 4—The Request for Proposal (RFP)

The RFP phase of the selection process is the most intensive and time-consuming phase. There are four key activities associated with this phase of work.

(1) Preparing the detailed functional and technical requirements for the system. This is usually broken out into key sections (discussed in previous chapters) providing details on the technology requirements, entity (performance center and asset) management, workflow and all the functionality associated with the core work and materials management modules as well as the support modules. This section of the RFP should also include the desired reporting tools and standard reports as well as the specifications for interfaces to existing and future business applications. A sample of CWMS functional requirements is provided in Appendix 8.6.

(2) Building a thorough RFP document. Your company's purchasing terms and conditions, vendor instructions for responding, overall CWMS selection process, RFP evaluation process, bid forms for response to both functional and cost items, together with the detailed functional requirements would constitute the complete RFP document. It is usually a good idea to have two separate responses to the RFP: one is the response to the technical proposal and the

other is the response to the cost items. The cost proposal should be submitted in a separate sealed envelope and should only be opened after the product demonstration phase of the selection process. This ensures that only cost proposals for products and vendors who meet the technical requirements would be opened and evaluated (serving to protect against extremely low bids that can skew the scoring in favor of poor technical responses). A sample RFP with the key headings is provided in Appendix 8.7.

(3) The bidders' meeting. When a large investment in a CWMS is being considered, it is recommended that a bidders' meeting be part of the selection process. This is usually scheduled early in the RFP response window and provides a face-to-face opportunity ensuring there is no doubt as to your requirements for a CWMS product and your partnership with the intended vendor. In addition, vendors get an opportunity to seek clarification in areas of the RFP that are not clear. It is important that minutes of this meeting are properly documented and circulated to all qualified bidders, together with any addenda to the RFP that may arise from the meeting.

(4) Evaluating the technical proposal. A scoring spreadsheet can be used to translate the responses to the RFP's technical requirements into a quantitative score. Each functionality (or requirement) is given a rating (based on priority) and also an importance for weighting. A weighted score (rating multiplied by importance) can then be computed for each requirement. A subtotal by section and grand total for each bidder can then be computed and analyzed to determine the ranking of bidders. This ranking is important to determine who should proceed to the product demonstration phase—usually the top two to three vendors and products are selected to move on to this phase.

Step 5—The Product Demonstration

This step is critical to validating the vendor's response to the RFP and evaluating how well the vendor meets your partnership requirements. It also gives a feel for the robustness and user friendliness of the system. It is essential that the vendor is given adequate instructions and time to prepare for the product demonstration. There should be clear instructions in the form of demonstrations script that serve to simulate the key (and critical) business processes to be enabled by the CWMS. There should be good background information on the typical users and sample data (asset, stock item, safety procedure, supplier, preventive maintenance job, customer ID) that represents your business environment. Similarly, instructions should be provided to the vendor to simulate your proposed technology environment (operating system, database, access to the Internet, interaction with office productivity tools, wireless access, printing). Finally, the vendor should be asked to present information on their company (company profile, staffing), extent of research and development, client and product support framework and implementation methodologies (configuration, interface development, system testing, data conversion, training). A scoring system should be prepared to evaluate the demonstration phase. This should focus on the following.

- validation of system functionality
- ease of use and robustness
- implementation methodologies
- ability to meet partnership requirements

The product demonstration should be able to help further rank the vendors short-listed from the RFP in terms of which vendor and product best meets your needs for a CWMS. This is important because further evaluation of the vendors at the contract negotiation stage may reveal that the number one candidate is not desirable for your company and you may need to move on to your second rank vendor. Sample demonstration scripts and scoring spreadsheet are given in Appendices 8.9 and 8.10, respectively. It should be noted that product demonstrations could be held either at your site or at the vendor's office. In the first case, your cost can be minimized (the vendor usually absorbs their cost as part of their sales process) and you also have the opportunity for additional personnel (other than your selection team) to observe the demonstration. This can help the buy-in process for the CWMS.

Step 6—Reference Evaluation and Contract Negotiations

There are a number of important preparatory activities to set the stage for the contract negotiations step. A phone interview should be conducted with all of the references that the vendors have identified in the RFP. (A sample check list of questions to be asked during the phone interview is given in Appendix 8.11). At times, based on the comfort level with the vendor, it may be necessary to visit a reference site and observe the system being used in live situations. (A sample site visit checklist is given in Appendix 8.12.) If everything checks out favorably, it is necessary to draw up a contract that sets the stage for a long and successful partnership with the vendor. You should seek legal advice to evaluate the software license and ensure that all dollar items, payment schedule, warranties, vendor personnel, scope items and schedules are clearly defined. It is advisable to have face-to-face discussions with the vendor at this stage. An experienced consultant acting on your behalf would be beneficial in this situation.

APPENDIX 8.1 SELECTION TEAM REQUIREMENTS

Core Team Members

(a) Work with the consultant to
   - develop functional requirements for the CWMS.
   - develop a request for information (RFI).
   - evaluate the responses to the RFI.
   - develop the request for proposal (RFP).
   - evaluate the responses to the RFP.
   - Develop the demo script.
   - Conduct demos.
   - Present recommendations to the steering committee based on
      —functional requirements.
      —RFI evaluation.
      —RFP evaluation.
      —demo evaluations.
      —vendor reference checks.
      —site visits.
      —vendor negotiations.
(b) Recommended Team Members
   - manager or person in authority with good overview of the business
   - union representative (preferably someone who can fill one of the roles identified below)
   - maintenance representative (any of the trades)
   - operations representative
   - materials management representative (stores/purchasing)
   - IT representative
   - consulting CWMS expert

Extended Team Members

(These members are involved as necessary to provide input into the process as well as communication to affected business units.)

- finance and administration representative
- engineering representative
- quality assurance and quality control
- laboratory representative
- safety officer

Team Members' Time Commitment

- core team—part-time based on the activities in the project schedule
- extended team—one to two days per discipline (to be interviewed by core team members)

Team Member Qualifications

- good understanding of their area of expertise (e.g., maintenance, operations, inventory, purchasing, accounting, budgeting, etc.)
- general understanding of the company's business
- basic computer literacy skills
- good team skills

Team Leader Qualifications

- good understanding of the company's business (vision, mission)
- good understanding of the company's policies and guidelines
- good understanding of the company's RFI/RFP process
- overall understanding of the work management and support business processes for the various areas of the company
- good computer literacy skills
- good project management skills
- background information on the CWMS project
- good leadership skills
- conflict and issue management skills

APPENDIX 8.2 KEY ELEMENTS OF THE PROJECT PLAN

The typical project plan for CWMS selection should be a word document that provides a clear guide for the selection process. The following topic areas are necessary.

- Introduction—provides background for the project, summarizes the business case, goals and objectives for the project and discusses overall scope and schedule.
- Selection team charter—this section provides a brief overview of the vision, mandate, roles, responsibilities, authorities, accountabilities and expected results from the team.
- Project team—a project team chart is usually desirable in this area, together with a discussion on team members' roles, time commitments and brief biographies.
- Selection methodology—this section discusses the methodology to be used for selecting the vendor and product that best meet the company's business needs.
- Work breakdown structures (WBS)—this section provides details on each of the major project activities (description, resourcing, time, scope, money, impact on the operations, dependencies with other activities), milestones and deliverables (both tangible and intangible). The WBS will be used to develop the project schedule.
- Quality control and quality assurance—this section should define the process for assuring quality in the selection process and provide clear guidelines on the quality control activities.
- Communication—provides an overview of the communication process for the selection phase and refers to the detailed communication plan (generally developed for the overall CWMS project).

APPENDIX 8.3 TEMPLATE FOR A COMMUNICATION PLAN

Audience (Who) (Examples provided)	Messages (What)	Interest of Audience (Why)	When	How/Deliverable	How Often/Who
Employees	Overall picture for the CWMS project and how it will achieve and sustain best in class operations. CWMS selection process	Staff needs to know how their work will be impacted by the CWMS project.	Ongoing during life of the project—specifically at key milestones	Tailgates, possible reports or newsletter for project	At key milestones and at least a monthly communication
Union	Overall picture for the CWMS project and how it will affect and improve their membership's work process and environment	The union needs to be aware of any potential changes that can affect negotiated items.	Ongoing during life of the project—specifically at key milestones	Tailgates, possible reports or newsletter for project	At key milestones and at least a monthly communication
Project Manager	Frequent project progress (time, scope, money), resource availability etc.	Responsible for successful delivery CWMS selection of the project, content for newsletter	Throughout the project, start to finish (at key milestones in both projects)	Project management meetings, e-mail, phone, presentation materials	Monthly progress meetings with project manager, planned sessions with other stakeholders
Project Sponsor	Major project milestones, major hurdles	Projected project timelines, implications for staff, licensing issues, cost/benefit analysis	Every month	Regular project management team meetings	Every month (CWMS team leader and consulting PM) Milestone-based Management staff, Executive management, Other departments, Board of directors, Council customers

APPENDIX 8.4 TEMPLATE FOR AN RFI

Topic Areas for the Request For Information (RFI)

(1) Introduction—provide a brief overview of your company's operations, current and future work philosophy, technology environment, organization structure and vision for the CWMS project.

(2) Scope of work for the project—give an overview of the CWMS functional and technical requirements and the desired services from the vendor.

(3) Project schedule—provide an overview of the major activities, anticipated duration, and resourcing requirements, together with major milestones.

(4) Vendor partnership—give your expectations of a business partnership with the vendor.

(5) General instructions to the interested vendor
   (a) Costs for RFI—to be incurred by the vendor
   (b) Submission process
   (c) Bidders' meeting
   (d) Subcontracting
   (e) Your company's general terms and conditions
   (f) Insurance
   (g) Indemnification

(6) RFI submission process—provide details on what is expected of the vendor when submitting their response to the RFI.

(7) RFI evaluation process—provide details on how all submissions will be evaluated (various areas and the points to be awarded). Take care to demonstrate that the evaluation process will be fair and unbiased.

APPENDIX 8.5 TEMPLATE FOR SCORING AN RFI

Focus Areas

(1) It is recommended that a combination of score and weighting system be employed. This is ideally suited for rating the different areas of the RFI that vary in importance, for example
   (a) each RFI item can have a score from 0 to 10.

    (b) each RFI item will also have a weight 0 to 5.

    (c) weighted score is the product of (a) and (b).

(2) Review all documentation submitted with the bid carefully (look at all demo CDs, brochures, etc.).

(3) Check for conformity with the submission requirements in the RFI and your company's purchasing terms and conditions. Any bid that does not meet your requirements should be discarded.

(4) Mandatory items—this approach requires that the vendor provide this software functionality, service or qualification in order for their submission to be considered. If this is not available, then the bid should be discarded.

(5) Use spreadsheet program to tally scores (sum scores of the individual scorers and compute an overall average).

(6) Arrange final scores in descending order. Identify five to eight vendors who best meet your requirements for the CWMS project and are found acceptable to move on to the request for proposal stage.

(7) Seek approval from your steering committee to proceed with the other selection phase activities for your short-listed vendors.

(8) Send out letters to all vendors you have chosen to move on to the request for proposal stage of the CWMS selection process.

(9) Send out "regret" letters to all vendors who did not meet your project requirements. Thank them for taking the time to prepare and submit a proposal on your RFI.

APPENDIX 8.6 TEMPLATE FOR FUNCTIONAL REQUIREMENTS DOCUMENT (FOR RFP)

Focus Areas

- Provide clear and concise information on the detailed functionality by module.
- Indicate if functionality is mandatory. (If the vendor does not provide it they will be excluded from the selection process.)
- Indicate the possible score and importance of the functionality.
- Provide a comments section in order for the vendor to provide additional details, if necessary.

Note: It is important that a numbering system for each module, major functionality and detailed functionality be developed and carried through to the remaining stages of the selection process. (This is critical for consistency and validation of the performance of the software.)

The following is a sample functional requirements document for one category and is provided as a guide.

Item No.	Description of Functionality	Possible Score	Weight	Maximum Score Possible	Comments
1.	Asset records				
2.	Performance centers				
3.	Work order management				
4.	Capital projects				
5.	Materials management				
5.1	Inventory				
5.2	Purchasing				
6.	Workflow				
7.	Asset management				
8.	Performance management				
9.	Financials				
9.1	Budgeting and general ledger				
9.2	Invoicing				
9.3	Accounts receivables				
10.	Document management				
11.	Permitting (safety)				
12.	Report writer				

APPENDIX 8.7 TEMPLATE FOR AN RFP

Topic Areas for the Request For Proposal (RFP)

This is generally very detailed, compared to the RFI.

(1) Introduction—provide a detailed overview of your company's op-

erations, current and future work philosophy, technology environment, organization structure and vision for the CWMS project.

(2) Scope of work for the project—give a detailed itemized description of the CWMS functional and technical requirements and the desired services from the vendor. Ensure that the table of items in this area identifies mandatory and optional items, the *weight* and *maximum possible* score together with a *comments* field.

(3) Project schedule—provide a detailed Gantt chart of the CWMS project activities, anticipated durations, and resourcing requirements together with major milestones. Ensure that your RFP requirements include the vendors' exceptions or suggested changes to the project schedule.

(4) Vendor partnership—give your expectations of a business partnership with the vendor for the selection, implementation phases and the life of the CWMS solution.

(5) General instructions to the short-listed vendors from the RFI stage

   (a) Costs for RFP—to be incurred by the vendor

   (b) Submission process (technical and cost proposals—ensure rates are submitted for the CWMS project life)

   (c) Period over which the bid would be valid

   (d) Bidders' meeting

   (e) Subcontracting

   (f) Your company's general terms and conditions

   (g) Your company's policies and requirements on collusions and conflict of interest

   (h) Format and details required on vendor qualifications (necessary to evaluate the vendor's financial stability and industry competitiveness)

   (i) Insurance requirements

   (j) Indemnification requirements

   (k) Requirements for reference checks and site visits

   (l) Vendor resources—all key resources to be used on the project must be named (e.g., project manager, business analyst, programmer)

   (m) Presentation and product demonstration phase requirements

   (n) Contract requirements

   (o) Minority- and women-owned business requirements (if applicable)

   (p) Insurance requirements

   (q) Payment process for software and services during the project

   (r) Description of your interpretation of "substantial compliance" by the vendor for the scope of work

   (s) Source code escrow requirements (safeguard in the event that the vendor goes out of business)

(6) RFP submission process—provide details on what is expected of the vendor when submitting their response to the RFP.

(7) RFP evaluation process—provide details on how all submissions will be evaluated, the various areas and the points to be awarded. Take care to demonstrate that the evaluation process will be fair and unbiased.

(8) Give notice of acceptance and an invitation to the presentation and product demonstration phase.

APPENDIX 8.8 TEMPLATE FOR SCORING AN RFP

Focus Areas

(1) A similar scoring method is recommended for the RFP: a combination of score and weighting system should be employed. This is ideally suited for rating the different areas of the RFP that vary in importance, for example

   (a) each RFP item can have a score from 0 to 10.

   (b) each RFP item will also have a weight 0 to 5.

   (c) weighted score is the product of (a) and (b).

(2) Unlike the RFI, the RFP submissions from the vendors will have a cost component. This can be handled in two ways.

   (a) If a two-envelope process is employed for the RFP (separate technical and cost submissions), then the technical submission can be valuated using the method suggested above. The cost proposals for those vendors whose technical bids are found to be acceptable are then ranked by dollar value and the lowest bid is selected. It is always a good idea to have your estimate to validate the soundness of the bids. (This can guard against collusion or ridiculously low bids that are a sure sign of problems in the future.)

   (b) Another equally acceptable method is to convert the dollars in the cost proposal into a score. Here, you have to make a determination of the amount of money that would be equal to one point. (You can set a minimum total dollar value, e.g., $1 million qualifies for 10 points and for every $200K over this figure, the vendor loses 1 point.) Each cost should have a weight based on level of importance in order to develop a weighted score for the cost proposal. This should then be incorporated into the weighted score for the technical proposal.

(3) Carefully review all documentation submitted with the bid (product specifications, comments on functionality items, reference claims, etc.).

(4) Check for conformity with the submission requirements in the RFP and your company's purchasing terms and conditions. Any bid that does not meet your requirements should be discarded.

(5) Mandatory items—this approach requires that the vendor provide this software functionality, service or qualification in order for their submission to be considered. If this is not available, then the bid should be discarded.

(6) Use a spreadsheet program to tally scores. (Sum scores of the individual scorers and compute an overall average.)

(7) Arrange final scores in descending order. Identify two to three vendors who best meet your requirements for the CWMS project and will be moving on to the presentation and product demonstration stage of the CWMS selection process.

(8) Seek approval from your steering committee to proceed with the other selection phase activities for your short-listed vendors.

(9) Send out letters to all vendors you have chosen to move on to the presentation and product demonstration stage of the CWMS selection process. (Remind these vendors of the preparatory requirements of this stage.)

(10) Send out "regret" letters to all vendors who did not meet your project requirements. Thank them for taking the time to prepare and submit a proposal on your RFP.

APPENDIX 8.9 TEMPLATE FOR A VENDOR PRESENTATION AND A PRODUCT DEMONSTRATION SCRIPT

Focus Areas

(1) Provide detailed instructions on how this phase will be conducted and evaluated.

(2) Provide sample data representative of your business so that the vendor can be prepared for the presentation and product demonstration (e.g., asset, inventory, vendor, specification, permit and user records, suggested reports).

(3) Develop work-related scenarios that will cover the key areas of your company's business (follow the key business practices identified in your "to be" processes—work management, materials management, capital projects, asset management, etc.).

(4) Cross-reference each step in the workflow for the business processes with the functionality identified in the RFP. (It would be necessary to cover all of the mandatory items as well as the key desirable items.) Use a similar numbering scheme as in the RFP.

(5) List the score and weight for each item. Provide a field for comments.

(6) Allow the vendor adequate time to present how they will meet your expectations of a successful business partnership. (Again, as in (3) above, list the sore and weight for each item.)

(7) Ensure that the vendor provides all hardware to be used in the presentation and demonstration (this includes bar-coding and mobile devices).

APPENDIX 8.10 TEMPLATE FOR A DEMONSTRATION SCRIPT SCORE SHEET

Focus Areas

(1) A similar scoring method is recommended for the presentation and product demonstration stage; a combination of score and weighting system should be employed. This is ideally suited for rating the different areas of this stage that vary in importance, for example
  (a) each RFP item can have a score from 0 to 10
  (b) each RFP item will also have a weight of 0 to 5.
  (c) weighted score is the product of (a) and (b).

(2) At the end of each scenario, your facilitator should ensure that all scorers understood, scored and were able to identify the RFP item that the demonstration cross-referenced.

(3) Mandatory items—if the vendor does not successfully show a mandatory item, the demo should be stopped and the vendor should be disqualified.

(4) Scorers should remain part of the selection process from the RFI to this stage—this would ensure that all subjectiveness of scorers is consistent throughout the process.

(5) Use a spreadsheet program to tally scores. (Sum scores of the individual scorers and compute an overall average).

(6) Arrange final scores in descending order. Identify the vendor that best meets your requirements for the CWMS project.

(7) Seek approval from your steering committee to proceed with the other selection phase activities for your top vendor.

(8) Send out a letter to the vendor identified for the reference and site visits.

(9) You should now proceed with reference checks and/or site visits, as necessary, in preparation for the vendor contract negotiation phase of the project.

(10) Send out "regret" letters to all vendors who did not meet your presentation and product demonstration requirements. Thank them for taking the time to participate in this stage of the selection process.

APPENDIX 8.11 REFERENCE EVALUATION CHECKLIST

General Information:

Client _____ Vendor _____ Product _____ Date installed _____

No. of concurrent users _____

Overall comments: _____

Item No.	Topic Areas and Questions	Person Interviewed (Position)	Rating (Good, Average, Poor)	Comments
1.	Did you use external help to select and implement the CWMS?			
2.	How would you rate the value provided by the consultant?			
3.	How long did the CWMS project take (selection to complete implementation)?			
4.	Can you quantify the costs and benefits from the CWMS project? How do they compare with the original business case?			
5.	Review the selection process.			
6.	Review the makeup of the CWMS teams (selection and implementation). How were the team dynamics?			
7.	Review the conference room pilot.			

(continued)

Item No.	Topic Areas and Questions	Person Interviewed (Position)	Rating (Good, Average, Poor)	Comments
8.	Review the data conversion and collection process.			
9.	Review the testing process.			
10.	Review the hardware deployment process—level of accessibility.			
11.	Review the communication plan. How effective was the process?			
12.	Review the CWMS support system.			
13.	Review the CWMS configuration management system.			
14.	What modules are currently in use?			
15.	Seek explanations for modules or functions not being used.			
16.	Describe the level of user friendliness and user acceptance.			
17.	Are you satisfied with the speed of the system at sign-on and during a typical query?			
18.	Describe the integrated technology solution. How is it managed?			
19	Review the level of use of CWMS data for decision making.			
20.	Review the reporting capability of the system. (What reports are available?)			

(continued)

Item No.	Topic Areas and Questions	Person Interviewed (Position)	Rating (Good, Average, Poor)	Comments
21.	What percentage of the database is populated by the various records:			
21.1	Asset			
21.1.1	Permits			
21.1.2	Drawings			
21.1.3	Specifications			
21.2	Inventory			
22.	Review the level of data quality and integrity.			
23.	Review the CWMS vendor performance.			
24.	Review the CWMS consultant performance.			
25.	Review business practice metrics related to the CWMS.			
25.1	Percentage proactive work			
25.2	PM compliance			
25.3	Schedule compliance			
25.4	Level of predictive work			
25.5	Inventory value			
25.6	Inventory turnover, etc.			

APPENDIX 8.12 SITE VISIT CHECKLIST

This is similar to the reference checklist, but would capture more details from face-to-face and on-site interactions.

General Information:

Site _____ Vendor _____ Product _____ Date installed _____

Personnel interviewed _____

Item No.	Topic Areas and Questions	Person Interviewed (Position)	Rating (Good, Average, Poor)	Comments
1.	Did you use external help to select and implement the CWMS?			
2.	How would you rate the value provided by the consultant?			
3.	How long did the CWMS project take (selection to complete implementation)?			
4.	Can you quantify the costs and benefits from the CWMS project? How do they compare with the original business case?			
5.	Review the selection process.			
6.	Review the makeup of the CWMS teams (selection and implementation). How were the team dynamics?			
7.	Review the conference room pilot.			
8.	Review the data conversion and collection process.			

(continued)

Item No.	Topic Areas and Questions	Person Interviewed (Position)	Rating (Good, Average, Poor)	Comments
8.	Review the data conversion and collection process.			
9.	Review the testing process.			
10.	Review the hardware deployment process—level of accessibility.			
11.	Review the communication plan. How effective was the process?			
12.	Review the CWMS support system.			
13.	Review the CWMS configuration management system.			
14.	What modules are currently in use?			
15.	Review system in use.			
15.1	Work order module			
15.2	Inventory module			
15.3	Purchasing module, etc.			
16.	Describe the level of user friendliness and user acceptance.			
17.	Quantify the speed of the system at sign-on.			
18.	Quantify the speed of the system for a typical query.			

(continued)

Item No.	Topic Areas and Questions	Person Interviewed (Position)	Rating (Good, Average, Poor)	Comments
19.	Describe the integrated technology solution.			
19.1.	Architecture			
19.2.	Interface requirements			
19.3.	Interface specifications			
19.4.	Interface unit testing process			
20.	How is the integrated solution managed?			
21.	Review the back-up and recovery process.			
22.	Review the level of use of CWMS data for decision making.			
23.	Review the reporting capability of the system. (What reports are available?)			
24.	What percentage of the database is populated by the various records:			
24.1.	Asset			
24.1.1	Permits			
24.1.2	Drawings			
24.1.3	Specifications			
24.2	Inventory			

(continued)

Item No.	Topic Areas and Questions	Person Interviewed (Position)	Rating (Good, Average, Poor)	Comments
25.	Review the level of data quality and integrity.			
26.	Review the CWMS vendor performance.			
26.1	System implementation			
26.2	System support (maintenance contract)			
26.3	Effectiveness of the end-user conference			
26.4	Effectiveness of the end-user group			
26.5	Level of R&D—product updates etc.			
27.	Review business practice metrics related to the CWMS.			
27.1	Percentage proactive work			
27.2	PM compliance			
27.3	Schedule compliance			
27.4	Level of predictive work			
27.5	Inventory value			

CHAPTER 9

Preparing to Implement a CWMS

Successful implementation of a CWMS requires a great deal of planning and use of resources, both internally as well as externally consultant and/or vendor. Careful preparation before the actual implementation activities can smooth the way for a successful project. Some of these activities can start before the end of the selection process. A high-level plan can be developed that identifies these as well as other key activities necessary for a successful implementation. The CWMS implementation process is shown in Figure 9.1. Only the preparation phase will be discussed in detail in this chapter, the remaining steps will be discussed in Chapter 10.

STEPS IN THE PRE-PLANNING PHASE OF THE IMPLEMENTATION PROCESS (FIGURE 9.2)

The activities in the pre-planning phase are: planning for change, developing the work plan and communications, developing supporting organization, developing hardware infrastructure, defining "to be" work processes and collecting preliminary data.

Step 1—Planning for Change and Selecting an Implementation Team

Planning for Change

Essentially a CWMS project is a change management process: the sig-

127

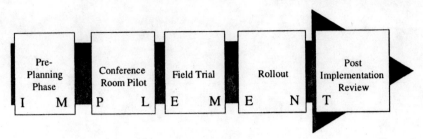

FIGURE 9.1 *CWMS Implementation Process.*

nificance of the change is usually very little if the project is a replacement of an existing system. The more popular CWMS projects are usually a first-time implementation. In this case, it means converting the entire work management process from a paper- or verbal-based system into one that is fully electronic. There is considerable fear of the unknown, therefore, a reluctance to relinquish a process that has been used for many years. Many end users have probably never used a computer so there is concern that they may be unable to learn the new technology, hampering their ability to do a good job. Some are afraid that the younger employees

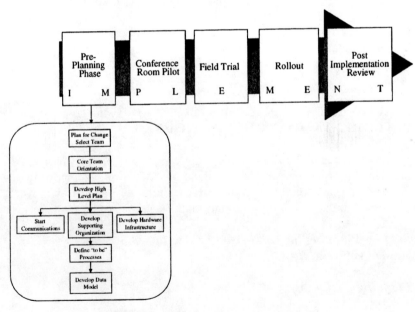

FIGURE 9.2 *Steps in the Pre-planning Phase.*

(who have come to embrace technology as part of life) would have an upper hand on them. In addition, many employees (especially unionized employees) are apprehensive that the CWMS is just another management tool to monitor their performance and the time they spend doing work in order to wring some more productivity from them. Some, who actually understand how the CWMS can be effective at taking control of work, are fearful that their inefficiencies over the years would be easily revealed. They would no longer be able to hide under the ad hoc systems and lack of documentation. Like any other change management process it is essential to recognize these concerns and be proactive in dealing with them. Change management techniques should be applied to prepare the organization for the major changes to come. It can be likened to "unfreezing" the organization, making the necessary changes, then "refreezing" the organization in the new way of doing business with the CWMS. This ensures that there is no backsliding into the old way of doing things. The following sections discuss some of the other preparatory work that can be done to help "unfreeze" the organization. Guidelines and suggestions for making the actual changes and "refreezing" the organization are discussed in Chapter 10—CWMS Implementation Methodologies.

Creation of an Implementation Team

In deciding on the size of the implementation team in line with the A to Z implementation concept, it is important that the appropriate balance of team members be considered. This means considering a small number of team members (for quick decision making and less impact on operations) with representation from all groups for consensus and buy-in. The latter, of course, leads to paralysis by analysis and an extremely long implementation process. Experience suggests that the most effective team arrangement is one with a small number (five, including the team leader) of core team members who can draw on the unique experience and knowledge of specific extended team members. The core team should have a direct reporting line through the team leader to the steering committee. Typical representatives for these positions are given in Figure 9.3.

Qualifications

- steering team
  - —executive sponsor for the CWMS (high enough level necessary to give adequate importance to the project)

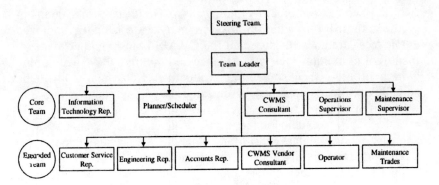

FIGURE 9.3 *Typical Selection Team Organization Chart.*

   —senior management staff from the various department and divi-
     sions that will be implementing the software
 • team leader
   —senior individual who understands the company's overall poli-
     cies and procedures (departmental as well as well as corpo-
     rate)
   —must have excellent: project management skills, facilitation
     skills, communication skills, leadership skills/interpersonal
     skills, computer skills (MS productivity tools as well as a basic
     understanding of technology)
   —desirable to have previously led multidisciplined teams
 • team members (would apply to extended team members also)
   —excellent understanding of area of expertise
   —previous work in a team setting
   —basic computer skills
 • CWMS consultant
   —experience in selecting and implementing various CWMS
   —familiarity with hardware and networking infrastructure design
     and deployment
   —work and asset management-related experience
   —materials management experience
   —project management experience
   —change management experience
 • CWMS vendor
   —successful implementation of the CWMS
   —programming expertise
   —client satisfaction

Roles and Responsibilities

- steering team—executive decision making, removal of policy related hurdles to implementation, visible endorsement and support for the program by reinforcing the benefits expected
- team leader—overall guidance and leadership for implementation; issue and conflict resolution; shared project management responsibility for project coordination, administration and management with the CWMS consultant and quality control and quality assurance for the project.
- team members—all activities associated with implementation in line with their areas of expertise (setting configuration parameters, collecting loading test data, system testing, training—to be discussed in detail in Chapter 10)
- extended team members—specialized input as needed based on their area of expertise
- CWMS consultant—advise and support team leader for the overall project, system configuration (shared with the vendor), definition of specifications, development of templates, setup of records, best practices input for configuration and performance metrics, customization of training materials from the vendor, delivery of training, go live preparedness checks, go live support.
- CWMS vendor—loading of software, core team training on the CWMS, system configuration, electronic data conversion, interface development, go live support

Time Commitment

CWMS implementation time can vary over a six-month to a three-year period, depending on the number of users, number of different departments, number of modules, extent of data collection and deployment of hardware infrastructure expected. In general, one year to one and one-half years is typical of most CMWS implementations for a user base of over 100. Long implementation periods are usually associated with problems (discussed in Chapter 13). It is important that the core implementation team is given adequate time to do a good job. This usually means undivided attention to the task at hand. It is not uncommon to find core team members being assigned to the project full time for the first six months for the conference room pilot (CRP) and field trial and then on a reduced basis in the subsequent rollout phase. The team leaders may be required to stay on full time until the system is fully rolled out and functional at all sites.

Communications

In the pre-planning step of implementation, there is a unique opportunity to prepare the user community by initiating relevant communication on the project. In order to start the CWMS selling process to users, a communications plan should be developed and implemented at this point in time. The various audiences, key messages, medium for communication, who delivers the message and when (how often) should be determined. A good job at this stage will help alleviate a lot of apprehension about technology, set the right expectations and pave the way for the much needed support for success. In general, one communication plan is developed for the overall selection and implementation phases of the project, the template discussed in Appendix 8.3 will apply is this area also.

Step 2—Core Team Orientation

The core team must be adequately prepared for the implementation process. The core team needs to understand the different phases of the implementation process and the various steps in each phase. They also need to be aware of their roles and responsibilities, authority and expected results. It would be very useful at this point to develop a team charter (a typical template is shown in Appendix 9.1) for the team that provides guidance over the course of implementation. In addition, the team must be given an orientation in conflict and issue resolution and shown how they can effectively use an issues log (typical issue log and framework shown in Appendix 9.2).

Step 3—Project Planning and Integration with Other Projects

Good planning is critical to meeting the project management metrics of project completion on time, within scope, within budget and with managed impact of the operations. The project plan should clearly identify the key activities by description, scope, sequencing, expected duration, resources required (external and internal), funding, interdependencies and deliverables. This information should then be summarized into a project schedule that supports the project management process and identifies key milestones throughout the project. A well thought out project plan will ensure that adequate resources, funding and time commitments are projected for the various activities and the critical path activities are identified. A good project plan can be used to provide all members with advance notice of the time demands on their services. As a tracking tool, the project schedule can drive the payment process for services (as well as software) received and allow for budget management by computing the estimate to complete for each activity at the end of any reporting period. In any CWMS implementation, demonstrated progress (achievement of milestones) and quick wins should be communicated in order to keep the excitement and momentum buoyant. (A template for developing a project plan and a sample project schedule is given in Appendix 9.3)

Step 4—Creation of an Organization to Support the CWMS

One pre-planning area that is usually forgotten is the support requirements for the implemented CWMS solution. Adding an additional business application to the technology environment together with interface programs, additional hardware and networking infrastructure will increase the support demands from the information technology group in the company. In many companies, this is usually the domain of a corporate IT group—get them involved up front and seek their commitment for the service level expected. Corporate IT should ensure that they incorporate the system backup and disaster recovery for the CWMS into their normal operations. Personnel should be trained to provide help-desk support and the CWMS solution incorporated into the system development life cycle concept (discussed in Chapter 6).

Step 5—Validate and Confirm, the "To Be" Business Processes to Support Configuration

In order to release any significant benefits from a CWMS implementation, the work management process for various work scenarios must be effective. There must be a good knowledge of current ("as is") work processes and the various scenarios for which they currently apply (e.g., emergency work related to a broken water main, preventive maintenance related to pumps, predictive maintenance related to motor control centers). The re-engineered business processes (or "to be" processes) in Chapter 2 should be validated at this stage and modified if necessary to support the configuration process. These "to be" work processes are the key inputs to the system configuration step (discussed in Chapter 10) and will provide the answers for populating CWMS business rules, tables, value lists and user-defined fields. In many cases this means validating that current practices are indeed best practices, identifying very ineffective processes (especially in a very reactive work environment) or identifying work processes that require minor tweaking to be in line with best practices standards. You may also consider redesign of a few major processes to get the CWMS implementation process going and then make incremental changes to the processes (and the CWMS configuration) on an ongoing basis. The intent of this book is not to provide guidance on how to re-engineer your processes, but rather identify that computerizing ineffective work processes will result in more inefficiencies. If a company intends to embark on a large scale re-engineering of work practices they should seek expert advice on this process. A typical "as is" and "to be" example (routine work) is given in Appendix 9.4.

Step 6—Develop the Hardware Infrastructure

In order to get a jumpstart on the implementation process, sometimes it is possible to do some preliminary work on the hardware and networking infrastructure. A good RFP would normally solicit recommendations from vendors on hardware and connectivity requirements for their CWMS based on proposed usage data (number of users, transactions, records, report requirements). This data will be very helpful in sizing and upgrading servers, PCs, printers and the network (WAN/LAN). In addition, if there is no available computer training area, secure a suitable room and install at least ten networked computers (with a printer) to the conference room pilot, field trial and rollout activities. This facility should be functional for loading of software to kick off the key project activities. Note that it is not necessary to install end-user hardware needed for the rollout step prior to the start of the conference room pilot.

Step 7—Develop the Data Model

This is a critical step in the pre-planning process and sets the stage for data flow based on transactions within the CWMS as well as data flow in the overall integrated technology solution. There are a number of different data modeling techniques and tools that can be used in the development of the data model. Some can be quite simple as in the case of standard office productivity tools (Visio) or very complex, requiring special expertise (e.g., Rational Rose, Rethink, Chaos). Key inputs into the modeling process are: the "to be" work processes, data and informational needs from other business (usually support groups such as finance) and performance management reporting requirements. The main outputs from the data model are system configuration workflows, data records design (e.g., the layout of the asset record with all the various tabs and data fields) and data flow and frequency requirements to support interface design.

On completion of the data model, you are now in a position to consider preliminary data collection in preparation for the conference room pilot and field trial processes. If the current data set for assets (description, serial numbers, specifications, procedures), stock items, MSDS sheets or, preventive maintenance jobs is incomplete, the pre-planning phase is an ideal opportunity to do some preliminary data collection. The first major decision for the implementation team will be to define the field trial area. This would allow focus of data collection efforts in this area of operations. In deciding the field trial area, the following criteria should apply.

- large enough to give a good representation of the user base and simulation of all the business functions
- small enough to allow the core implementation team to be able to quickly gather all the data for the production database and deploy the necessary hardware
- small number of users to get training done as quickly as possible
- business processes well understood and practiced
- realization of field trial area management team that CWMS is an important tool to support work management—willing champions for the system
- high likelihood of success

The vendor can be very helpful at this stage in identifying all the possible data fields for the various relevant records in the CWMS. This can be used to develop suitable data collection templates to be filled out by the data collectors. Data collection can consist of a number of activities—actual visits to assets in the field (if they are accessible), review of old paper records, validation of data with manufacturers if there is any doubt as to specifications. Data collection can be done on a daily basis as part of normal operations (crews working around specific assets are asked to fill out the data template) or a dedicated small team of data collectors can be trained up and give full-time responsibility for the data collection task. The method adopted will depend on the availability of resources as well as the urgency for the data in the implementation process. At times it may be necessary to hire external help to expedite data collection when resources are scarce and there is a short time frame for the field trial and overall rollout of the system. All data should be converted to an electronic format. This can be a spreadsheet or simple database to facilitate easily upload to the CWMS database at the appropriate time.

APPENDIX 9.1 CWMS TEAM CHARTER

Areas To Be Defined in the Team Charter

- team name and project name (usually something catchy and enduring)

- team members (List all core and extended team members.)
- vision of the CWMS project
- goals and objectives of the team
- team mandate (clear statement on what the team is expected to do)
- roles (Describe the specific roles to be played by the team members.)
- responsibilities (Describe the specific responsibilities for each role.)
- authorities (Describe the authority of the team and team leader.)
- deliverables (List the key deliverables and time frame.)
- milestones (List the major milestones—key events to be celebrated.)
- accountabilities (Identify the various groups the team is accountable to and what they are accountable for.)
- accountabilities (Identify the various groups that are accountable to the team and what they are accountable for.)

Use of the Team Charter

- orientation of team—kick-start the team-building process
- ongoing validation for the team during the progress of the project (being on track with the sponsor's objectives)
- aids in regaining a sense of purpose when "lost in the weeds"
- a great way to help with the communication process to the wider CWMS community

APPENDIX 9.2 TEMPLATE FOR CWMS IMPLEMENTATION TEAM ISSUES LOG

No.	Description of Issue	Priority	Status	Date Raised	Date Closed	Aging (Days)	By Who	Action By	Comments
1.	Need to install LAN at CWMS pilot site.	1	Open	June 19, 2003		30	Joe Bloe	Network coordinator	Specifications developed; job is being tendered out; expected completion date, September 30, 2003
2.	Prepare dedicated CWMS conference room pilot area with 12 networked PCs, server, printer, and telephone.	1	Closed	April 01, 2003	June 19, 2003	100	Jack Straw	Facilities manager	Facilities completed; computer equipment tested out; security system installed and facilities handed over to CWMS core team
3.	CWMS team members would like to be paid "mileage" to work at CWMS CRP site.	2	Open	April 01, 2003		100	Team members	Team leader	Discussed with HR—benefit does not apply; issue raised with director O&M

Priority - 1 (highest) to 4 (lowest)
Status - open or closed
Aging - automatically calculated by spreadsheet cell formula
Comments section - track progress and conclusion

APPENDIX 9.3 IMPLEMENTATION PROJECT
PLAN AND SCHEDULE

The typical project plan for a CWMS Implementation project should be a word document that provides a clear guide for the implementation process. The following topic areas are necessary.

- introduction—provides background for the project, summarizes the business case, goals and objectives for the project and discusses overall scope and schedule.
- Selection team charter—this section provides a brief overview of the vision, mandate, role, responsibilities, authorities, accountabilities and expected results from the team.
- Project team—a project team chart is usually desirable in this area, together with a discussion on team members' roles, time commitments and brief biographies.
- Implementation methodology—this section discusses the methodology to be used for selecting the vendor and product that best meet the company's business needs.
- Work breakdown structures (WBS)—this section provides details on each of the major project activities (description, resourcing, time, scope, money, impact on the operations, dependencies with other activities), milestones and deliverables (both tangible and intangible). The WBS will be used to develop the project schedule (Figure A9.3.1).

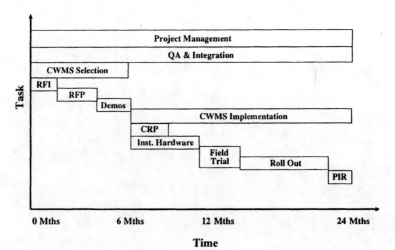

FIGURE A9.3.1 *Typical Project Schedule (Gantt Chart).*

- Quality control and quality assurance—this section should define the process for assuring quality in the selection process and provide clear guidelines on the quality control activities.
- Communication—provides an overview of the communication process for the selection phase and refers to the detailed communication plan (generally developed for the overall CWMS project).

APPENDIX 9.4 "AS IS" AND "TO BE" WORK PROCESS FLOW CHARTS FOR "ROUTINE WORK"

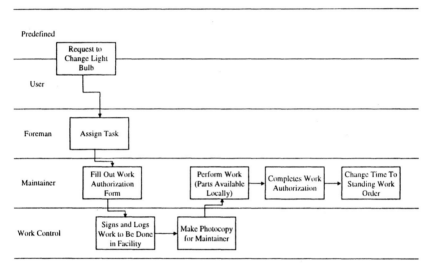

FIGURE A9.4.1 *"As Is" Work Process Flow Chart for "Routine Work."*

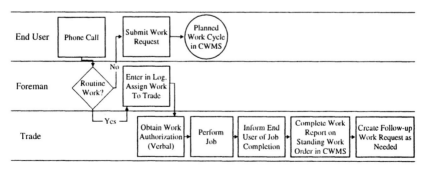

FIGURE A9.4.2 *"To Be" Work Process Flow Chart for "Routine Work."*

CHAPTER 10

CWMS Implementation Methodologies

Implementing a CWMS is very similar in concept to the selection process. You are again faced with the big dilemma of using consulting help or doing it yourself (the A to Z concept shown in Figure 10.1). Similar to the selection process, many companies have tried to implement a CWMS internally and have not been successful, partly because of lack of experience, lack of resources and a lack of sponsorship within the organization for the project. Conversely, many companies have spent untold fortunes on consulting fees to implement a CWMS and have many horror stories to tell about the experience. The following diagram (Figure 10.1) depicts the A to Z implementation concept.

Essentially, implementation (as well as selection) can be viewed as a continuum. At one end of the spectrum, a consultant is hired to do everything on behalf of the client with minimal involvement by client employees. At the other, the client undertakes the entire project in-house with very little external (consulting and vendor) support. Both approaches are fraught with problems. In the first example, using external resources can result in a quick implementation process and incorporation of best in class practices, but is usually very costly, allows for very little knowledge transfer to in-house staff and poor system acceptance by users. In the second example, there can be a low-cost project with a high level of buy-in and ownership but it is usually time-consuming and the existing work processes are generally duplicated. This means that if work is done by poor work management using a paper-based process, after implementing the CWMS, work is done by a poor work management process using a computer and software! The obvious solution is a mix of external and internal resources to create a cost-effective solution that incorporates best

141

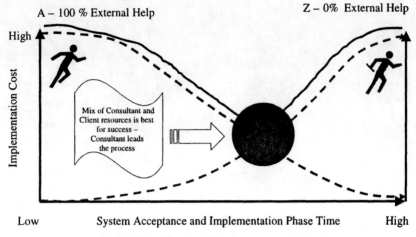

FIGURE 10.1 *The A to Z Implementation Concept.*

in class work processes. In addition, the knowledge transfer concept (Figure 10.2) discussed at the selection stage is also very applicable in this situation. A comfortable balance can usually be found in using external CWMS experts to partner with staff and vendor support personnel. As the implementation moves on to the rollout phase, adequate knowl-

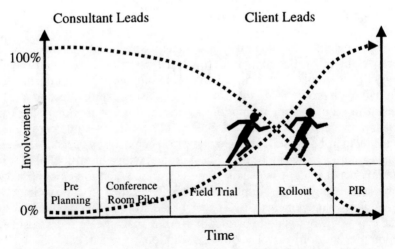

FIGURE 10.2 *Implementation Methodology Maximizes Knowledge Transfer.*

edge transfer should have occurred in order for staff to take a lead role in this phase.

THE CWMS IMPLEMENTATION PROCESS PHASES

Conference Room Pilot Phase

The conference room pilot (CRP) is the term used to describe the phase of system development and testing prior to a field trial of the software with real users. In this phase, the implementation core team will review the project plan from the pre-planning phase and create the necessary details to manage this phase effectively. The steps in the CRP phase are shown in Figure 10.3.

Step 1—Setup Conference Room Pilot Area

Usually the CRP is conducted in a dedicated room that is designed to allow the core team to have individual access to PCs and comfortable working space. In addition, it should be able to function as a training facility to provide classroom space as well as hands-on training to end users. The room should therefore be equipped with networked PCs (8 to 12) connected to the company's WAN, printer, white boards, data projector,

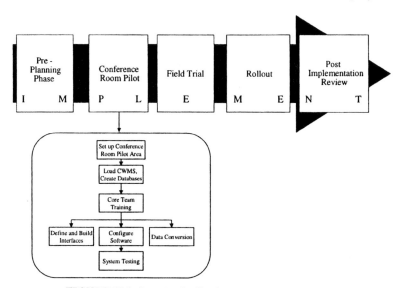

FIGURE 10.3 *Steps in the Conference Room Pilot Phase.*

bookcase and telephone access. The room should be secure to protect the hardware, software and work of the core team. When designing and selecting the CRP room, it should be kept in mind that this venue will be used during the field trial and rollout process. In the event that there is currently no such facility, then it would be a good idea to keep it, after the implementation, as a training room and for any work associated with the system development life cycle discussed in Chapter 6.

Step 2—Load CWMS Software and Create Database Instances

After the CRP venue is prepared, the next step is to load the CWMS software on an appropriate server (this could be located in the CRP room or at another site) and create the various copies of the database needed for the configuration. At least three instances (or copies) of the CWMS database should be created with suitable access to the core team members. There should be an original (pristine) production database, a test database, a development database and a training database. The production database should only be populated with data that you are absolutely sure is accurate and ready for going live (this is done towards the end of the CRP). The test database is the playground for the core team as they learn and experiment with configuration options. The development database is the repository of data and configuration decisions for final testing before transferring to the production database. The development database should be populated with data necessary to simulate redesigned business processes. The training database usually comes with the software from the vendor or can be a copy of the populated development database and is used for training of end users. The vendor's consultant or your CWMS consultant will be of immense help in this area.

Step 3—Core Team Training

In order for the core team to be adequately prepared for the conference room pilot phase of implementation (and indeed the entire implementation process), they must be given orientation on relevant best practices concepts, trained on the system and provided with "train the trainer" skills. Core team training therefore falls into three major categories:

(1) Best practices orientation—the core team needs to understand best practices around work (concepts discussed in Chapter 2), operations, asset management and performance management. The

CWMS consultant should provide this training; all training materials should be customized to reflect your industry and work environment.

(2) CWMS software training—the core team should be given training on the basic and advanced functionality of all the CWMS modules. This should then be followed by training on configuration setup and report generation.

(3) Train the trainer—the core team will be required to take a lead role in any end-user training. They should be given specific training in adult learning techniques with special emphasis on working with front line employees who are not exposed to computers or accustomed to long stints in classrooms.

Step 4—Configure Software

System configuration is the most significant step in the CRP phase. This is where you set business rules, develop the performance center hierarchy (parent-child relationships), populate list of values, tables and user-defined fields that replicate your manual and verbal business processes. You should be replicating "to be" business processes defined in the pre-planning phase discussed in Chapter 9. The most important business process is, of course, the work management process. During system configuration workflow parameters are also defined to enable the appropriate flow of transactions associated with business processes (in particular, the work order and materials management processes). Workflow parameters may be funds authorization limits associated with work orders, purchase requisition and purchase orders. In addition, workflow can be related to electronic prompts to requisitioners, or planners and schedulers when materials arrive at the stores. It is important that the CWMS consultant provides input into the configuration process based their experience with best practices associated with your business processes.

One of the most important areas that should form the basis for configuration for the work order process is the reactive, proactive and optimized work model. The discussion in Chapter 2 on best practices would prove very useful in the core team's configuration activities in this area. In addition, the core team needs to have a clear understanding of what is planned and unplanned work. Essentially, the only unplanned work is emergency work. (In this scenario, all efforts are very reactive and is focused on containing the situation protecting life and property.) Usually work is low cost and a high percentage is labor. (All follow-on work to rebuild should be planned—we do know that people continue to use the urgency created by the emergency as the excuse not to plan the follow-on work.) Other than emergency work, all other work should be properly planned. This means that there should be no category of work in your configuration that should be "planned" or "unplanned." The following work categories are recommended for configuration.

- category—reactive work
  —subcategory—emergency work (unplanned)
  —subcategory—breakdown (planned)
- category—proactive (all planned)
  —subcategory—time-based PM (calendar or run hours)
  —subcategory—upgrade back to original condition
- category—optimized (all planned)
  —subcategory—predictive PM
  —subcategory—corrective maintenance (from predictive PM)
  —subcategory—modification based on continuous improvement recommendations

One of the most common mistakes in configuration is the tendency to classify all work as either planned or unplanned. Towards the end of the configuration step, the core team should start working on customized reports that are necessary for performance management related to the work management process. Note that all of the work in the configuration step should be done on the test database.

Step 5—Data Collection and Conversion

In order to be able to evaluate if the configuration decisions would be able to support proposed business processes, it is necessary to populate the various records in the CWMS with representative data. This can be done through data collection and manual entry, or, in the event that you already have electronic records (existing CWMS or standalone databases), data conversion. The core team should identify which fields must be populated for the various CWMS records and develop suitable templates that can be used by the core team to conduct sample data from the field. They may also solicit help from field staff for this task. If data conversion is deemed feasible, then a data mapping exercise should be carried out where fields in the CWMS records are mapped to the equivalent fields in the other database; data conversion programs should then be developed to copy the records into the CWMS test database.

Step 6—Define and Build Interfaces

Interfaces and the concept of considering the CWMS as part of an integrated technology solution were discussed in Chapter 6. At this stage, the interfaces that are considered necessary for the field trial must be defined and the specifications determined, based on the type and frequency of data transfer between the CWMS and the existing business applications. Data transfer can be real time (changes in data in one system instantaneously duplicated in the other), near real time (a delay of a few seconds deemed to be acceptable), batch (daily, weekly, monthly) and ad hoc (interface run as needed).

Interface development will depend on choice of integration platform either directly from the CWMS to the other business applications or indirectly through an intermediary platform (sometimes called a "middleware"). The middleware facilitates the agent broker concept for data transfer. Many information technology professionals prefer this method because it provides more flexibility over direct interfaces for an integrated technology solution. Developing interfaces is one of the more complex tasks associated with a CWMS implementation and requires software programming experience and technical skill. Knowledge of both the CWMS and target application programs would be essential to successful interfaces development. Usually, external resources (CWMS expert or vendor consultant) will take the lead role for this task. Once all interfaces are developed, the development team must test them before the interfaces are applied to the test database—this process is usually called "unit testing" in the programming world.

Step 7—Conduct System Testing

On completion of steps 1 to 6, the CWMS test database is now ready to support the full testing of the CWMS. Before testing can be done, the core team must develop test scripts that simulate all the business processes to be enabled by the CWMS module. The demonstration scripts developed for the selection process would be an excellent starting point for developing the test scripts. Testing is usually carried out in two stages: modular testing and integrated testing:

- Modular testing refers to the testing of functionality and performance of the individual modules of the CWMS and also across modules. For example, testing the ability to create a work request and planning a work order from it (work order module).

Testing across modules would take this further by electronically creating purchase requisitions and purchase orders (purchasing module) and making demands from inventory (inventory module) in the support of the work order process.

• Integrated testing refers to the working of the CWMS with other business applications (in fact, this is testing of the interface programs). For example, paying for salaries, goods and services used in the process of doing work. It is important to ensure that the right dollar amounts in the form of journal entries are transferred from the CWMS to the financial system to the appropriate general ledger accounts for estimated and committed amounts. Conversely, when salaries and invoices are paid in the payroll and financial system, it is important to ensure that these amounts show up as actuals in the CWMS cost-reporting structure against the right performance centers.

The testing stage is iterative as the core team makes changes to the configuration decisions based on test results. In addition, you may identify "software bugs" that the vendor needs to correct. Try to conduct as many tests as possible to evaluate system performance and robustness. In addition, it is advisable to bring a few end users to evaluate the level of user friendliness of the system. These should be employees from the field trial area selected in the pre-planning phase discussed in Chapter 9. This could provide insights into changes that may make the systems more readily acceptable to end users. A template for a typical test plan is given in Appendix 10.1.

At the end of the CRP, all configuration parameters should be exported into the development database in preparation for the field trial phase of implementation. This should only be done when the core team is confident that the system configuration is acceptable and testing has revealed that the software is stable and robust.

Field Trial Phase

Some work has already been done on the field trial area in the previous phases—it was selected in the pre-planning phase and some employees were exposed to the software in the CRP phase. It is now time to develop the production database for the field trial area in preparation for go live with the CWMS. The steps in the field trial process are given in Figure 10.4.

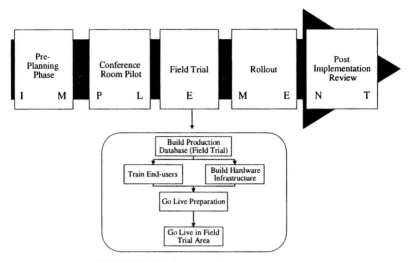

FIGURE 10.4 *Steps in the Field Trial Phase.*

Step 1—Data Collection, Conversion and Migration

The key areas of data collection are focused on development of production database records. The following is a listing of the various records to be developed.

- performance center hierarchy (or the entity structure)
  - —asset components at the lowest level (only necessary if work and cost history will be applicable at this level)
  - —followed by assets, asset locations and then the performance centers as per your business requirements (e.g., work areas, sections, divisions, departments up to the company level)
  - —specifications for each asset
  - —standard operating procedures (SOPs) for each process and asset
  - —drawings [assembly drawings for assets, process and instrumentation drawings (P&ID)]
  - —bill of materials for assets
- users with appropriate system access as per their roles in the various business areas
- financial data: general ledger codes, vendor records—payment information
- stock item records
- warehouse records—stock item vendor records

- permit information—procedures for confined space entry, lock and tag out, excavation, hot work
- purchasing records—vendor ordering information, standard terms and conditions
- any other records that may be necessary

It is obvious that there is a lot of data collection to be done at the field trial phase. In fact, this step requires the most effort in this phase. The good news is that for many companies most of this information may already be captured in electronic form or easily available in paper form. The data mapping and conversion task discussed previously should be applied here. Sometimes the integrity of your electronic data may be questionable and it may be advisable to conduct "data scrubbing" before it is transferred into the development database. Many companies who have embarked on CWMS projects have realized at this step that the data is of such poor quality that it is better to start fresh with data collection in the field, following appropriate quality assurance and control procedures. (Note in field data collection, data collectors should enter all data into templates and then into electronic spreadsheets. This allows for easy data quality control before the data is electronically converted into the development database.)

Step 2—Preparation of End-User Training Materials

While data collection is being conducted, the core team should be developing training materials for end users in the field trial. These materials must be adapted from the standard materials provided by the vendor and must reflect your business's unique needs. A brief orientation on relevant best in class practices and some rationale for the CWMS (how it helps the company and how it helps the end user) would be important to setting the context for the field trial. Training documentation must be simple and should have liberal "screen scrapes" of the actual PC screens that would be seen on the CWMS. The training database should be made by copying the development database when all configuration and field trial records are entered into this database. All CWMS records must be familiar to the end users (e.g., assets usually worked on, similar stock items). All training materials must be simple, with appropriate "cheat sheets" made available to end users for reference after training.

Step 3—Set Up End Users

Users must be set up with appropriate access for all of the functions they will be expected to use during the training. The user profiles should also be exactly like what they are expected to have during the live field trial. The core team members should ensure that the screens for users must be limited only to information that they would use during normal work. Excess information only serves to confuse and detract from the training. It is extremely important that core team members do many dry runs of the training to ensure that the users' profiles, passwords and CWMS functionality work as planned. Any stumbling by trainers, sign-on and system problems will only cement the views of the unwilling that the CWMS is difficult to use and would be a chore rather than a help to their work.

Step 4—End-User Training

Each user must have a dedicated PC during training and the class sizes must be chosen so as to provide as much individual attention and "hand holding" as possible during the training session. Your training room set up for the CRP will pay big dividends at this point. In structuring the training agenda, allow for many breaks; it may be worthwhile to consider having meals brought in. Ensure that the training room environment is conducive to comfortable learning. The goal is to make training as enjoyable as possible for adults who have spent most of their work life in the field environment. Training should be timed for completion as close as possible to go live in order to limit the amount of loss of knowledge before the new skills are used. The only remaining activity for the core team after end-user training should be go live preparation.

Step 5—Go Live Preparation and Go Live

Preparing for go live is a critical step in the implementation process. It requires a thorough check to ensure that everything is in place before end users are asked to start using the CWMS to support work management and the other business processes. Go live preparation can vary depending on whether the company has existing business applications or a manual process that will be replaced by the CWMS. In the first instance, it is necessary to determine if old systems will be run in parallel for some period of time together with the CWMS. Parallel testing will be used to decide when the old systems will be shut down. In the latter case, there will be little fear by end users of losing valuable business information and it is usually the easier go live for the core team. The following are the key areas that should be on a go live preparedness checklist.

- Production database is made by making a copy of the completed development database (all necessary records are in place and of good quality).
- All user profiles and passwords are set up and tested to be O.K.
- All CWMS functionality to be used in the field trial area has been tested to be O.K.
- All CWMS reports have been run and meet requirements.
- All hardware has been deployed and tested to be functional (servers, PCs, printers, mobile devices).
- All employees in the company are aware of the go live date and are aware of their roles and responsibilities.
- The end-user support framework is in place (help desk, issues log, onsite support logistics).
- A contingency plan is in place in the event that the system goes down (use of paper records etc.).
- System backup and recovery procedures are in place and tested.
- All static dynamic data (e.g., balance on hand for stock items) is electronically converted.
- All paper records needed for transactions (e.g., POs not received, live work orders, work requests, stock item balance on hand) on go live date are manually entered into the system immediately before go live. Note that all this should be done over a weekend or during a night shift when very few transactions are being generated. This means that the best go live date is on a Monday morning or at the start of the financial month.

If all of the above items check out to your satisfaction, then you can be assured of a relatively smooth go live of the CWMS in the field trial area. The core team should provide dedicated on-site support for at least a couple of weeks; carefully identifying, evaluating and correcting all issues on the go live issues log together with the CWMS and the vendor consultant. Any deficiencies identified as a result of end-user training should be noted and addressed both in terms of the training materials as well as the training process and agenda. Any configuration issues should be rectified ensuring that all changes are suitably documented in the configuration records for the CRP. Any deficiencies in data should also be noted and all data collection templates updated prior to the rollout phase. Similarly, any software or interface "bugs" should be promptly rectified by the vendor; or at least seek their commitment to have the correction as a software patch or in the next release of the software. The core team should work closely with the management team for the field trial area to track the extent of usage, system performance and quality of data being captured in the course of doing work during the support period.

ROLLOUT

Once the field trial is under way and performing well, the core team should start directing their attention to the rollout phase of implementation with the goal of duplicating the field trial successes in all areas of the company's operations. The steps in the rollout phase are shown in Figure 10.5. They are very similar to the field trial but on a much larger scale. Rollout of the CWMS to the various other business units can be done on a sequential or phased basis, or resources, permitting a big bang approach to all areas at one time.

Step 1—Prepare Detailed Rollout Plan

The type of rollout decided will set the stage for development of a detailed work plan to be used as a road map by the core team in implementing the software in all business units. This plan should consider realistic availability of resources to carry out the tasks associated with rollout. In addition, there is a need to consider the impact on the operations, as end users are co-opted for data collection activities and for CWMS training.

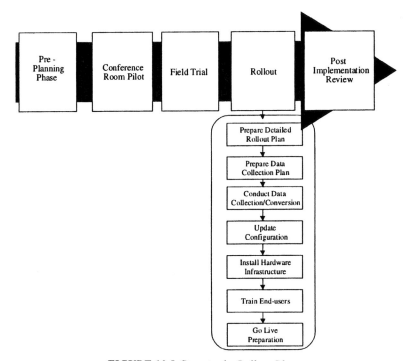

FIGURE 10.5 *Steps in the Rollout Phase.*

The answers to these concerns will dictate the time frame for completing the rollout of the CWMS. If CWMS and vendor consultants are involved, then the scope of their work and the budget should be clearly identified, together with the deliverables expected from them. Successful project management at this stage will be measured in terms of how well the core team meets the times, scope, budget and facility impact expectations of the steering team. The core team must also focus on timely communication (leveraging successes of the field trial) in order to prepare the other business areas for the CWMS.

Step 2—Prepare Data Collection/Conversion Plan

Data collection and conversion is the most extensive and tedious task in the rollout phase. It has the potential to consume a lot of resources and must be carefully managed. This task can get going as soon as the field trial goes live. A detailed data collection and conversion plan should be developed, focusing on capturing all of the static data (data that does not change with work-related transactions) and then timing the capture of dynamic data (data that changes with transactions on an ongoing basis) just prior to go live. As in the case of the field trial, a good quality assurance and control framework must be in place to ensure there is good data integrity.

Step 3—Update System Configuration

Field trial results may dictate the need for some configuration changes. In addition, there may be unique business needs of the other business areas that must be reflected in the configuration of the CWMS. All of these changes and new configuration items must go through the same process as in the CRP where rigorous testing must be done to ensure that all business processes can work smoothly on the CWMS. Data collection or mapping templates must be updated to reflect the additions or changes to the configuration. Similarly, the end-user training materials must be suitably adjusted. There may be a need for additional interfaces or modifications to the existing interfaces. A similar process should be followed to develop, test and apply all of these new interfaces. All additions and changes must be documented in the configuration and interfaces manuals.

Step 4—Install Hardware Infrastructure

Usually at the end of the CRP phase you would have a clear idea of the hardware and networking requirements for rollout of the CWMS to all areas of the operations. This task can require significant investment in funds if existing infrastructure is inadequate. Effective planning is essential for good phasing of expenditure of funds in the upgrading of the network infrastructure, new PCs and laptops (some may be ruggedized for industrial use), printers, servers and mobile computing devices [pen tablets, personal digital assistants (PDAs)].

Step 5—Train End Users

End-user training should be timed for completion just prior to go live of the CWMS in the various areas. All of the ideas discussed for end-user training at the field trial stage would certainly apply at this stage. The challenge, of course, is to provide effective training for so many users in a short time frame and also be geared up to provide follow-up training if necessary. It is a good idea at this stage to identify a few individuals from each business as CWMS champions (or "go to" people when the CWMS is live). These individuals should be given more detailed training (including some exposure to the train-the-trainer concepts that the core team experienced early on in the implementation process. Many CWMS vendors provide training materials as tutorials in their "help" feature. In addition, you may want to consider deploying all of your customized training materials on your company's intranet for easy accessibility to end users. In this way, they can be easily updated as you make ongoing changes to the system, or take advantage of new releases to the software by the CWMS vendor.

Step 6—Go Live Preparation and Support

All of the items listed under go live preparation and support in the field trial stage would be just as applicable in rollout, except on a bigger scale. There would be a need for a lot of planning and coordination, leveraging the help of the management teams for the various business units as well as the champions identified during the training step. Proper communication is essential to preparing all end users for the go live milestone. Everyone should be aware of the various avenues they could turn to for help if they have such a need during go live. There should be dedicated core team, CWMS and vendor consultant support for a few weeks, then reducing to support as necessary as the rollout becomes successful.

The Post Implementation Review

The last step in the CWMS implementation process is to conduct a post implementation review (PIR). This is often the step that is never carried out by most companies. Many people assume that everything will be fine once you switch on the system and go live. As in many change management projects, it is important to seek continuous improvement and reinforce new and desired behaviors. The PIR should be conducted by a small group of individuals selected from the core team and user groups. Your CWMS consultant should facilitate the PIR. The PIR is a key step in the change process to ensure that you are able to reap the benefits from the CWMS investment. The steps in the PIR are given in Figure 10.6.

Step 1—Review Configuration

A review of the current configuration in line with the desired business practices should be carried out. Any gaps identified should be noted and channeled through the change request process. (Any urgent changes should be done as soon as possible.)

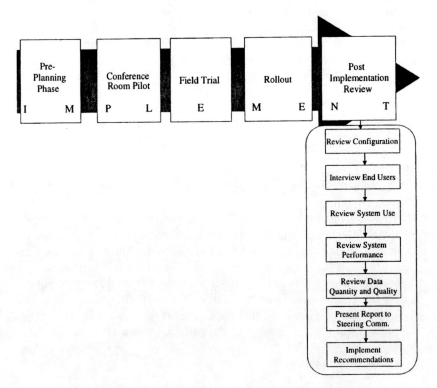

FIGURE 10.6 *Steps in the Post Implementation Review Phase.*

Step 2—Interview End Users

Carefully structured questions and observations of end-users using the system to conduct their various business processes would yield a lot of important information for fine tuning the CWMS. This may lead to adjusting user profiles to adding or limit accessibility, adding additional user-defined fields, modifying or creating new reports and identify missing data.

Step 3—Review System Use

A review of transaction logs, reports, inventory transactions, PRs and POs will indicate the extent of use of the system. Performance metrics (such as WR and WO backlogs, PM and schedule compliance) would also give an indication of the return on the CWMS investment.

Step 4—Review System Performance

This step refers to measuring the response of the system during peak and normal conditions. The time taken to log on to the CWMS, create records, run reports, run transactions, run interfaces and execute the various workflow components should be measured and compared with projections obtained from the vendor at the RFP stage. These measures should also be compared with the performance of other business applications in the company. Problems in this area could be attributable to connectivity, database or software configuration issues.

Step 5—Review Data Quantity and Quality

The PIR team should review the average increase in asset records (as new assets are added) and any type of records that are typically created during the work order process. These can be WRs, WOs, permits, PRs, POs, inventory receipts, pick lists or PM and can give an indication of how well the system is being used to support business processes. The quality of this data should be checked and any concerns should be promptly addressed. The goal is to nip data quality problems in the bud before the entire database becomes corrupted and there is little trust in the data.

Step 6—Present Report to Steering Team

The PIR team should develop a proper report for presentation to the steering committee. This should include findings, conclusions and recommendations associated with the CWMS implementation. The report should provide the first cut at the benefits tracking for the CWMS investment (based on the business case). The report should also provide costing and an implementation plan for the recommendations.

Step 7—Implement Recommendations

Once the steering team gives the green light, the PIR team may oversee implementation of the short-term recommendations, or, these should be assigned to volunteers from the core team. Medium and long-term recommendations should be referred to the system development life cycle process discussed in Chapter 6.

CONCLUSION

As a final note on implementation, the steering team, selection and implementation teams should be recognized for a successful project. In addition, the information learned from this process should be applied to other software selection and implementation projects.

APPENDIX 10.1 TEMPLATE FOR CWMS TEST PLAN

(1) Create a test map (using a spreadsheet program) with
   (a) test scenarios by functionality and module.
   (b) test scenarios between modules.
   (c) test scenarios.
   (d) expected results for each test.
(2) Develop user and data records to simulate the tests described above.
(3) Check and finalize system configuration necessary for conducting the testing.
(4) Develop instructions for testers.
(5) Conduct testing for each area following the scenarios, noting the following.
   (a) Full success and repeatable at least three times
   (b) Partial success (not repeatable)
   (c) Failure—did not work at all
(6) Capture the issues in a testing log and resolve testing results based on the following.

(a) Data issues—core team and consultant attention

(b) Testing setup issues—core team and consultant attention

(c) Software problems (bugs)—vendor attention

(d) Interface program issues—core team, consultant and vendor attention

(7) On correction of the issues, retesting should occur and the above process should be followed.

CHAPTER 11

Using the CWMS for Cost-Effective Work Management and Improved Equipment Reliability

After going through a detailed process on how to select the right CWMS for your business and then showing you the steps for successful implementation; it may come as a surprise that changing to a best in class operations is really more dependent on the practices. The results will depend on how you use the technology solution to support your business practices to achieve cost-effective work management and improved asset reliability. Best in class work management practices were discussed in Chapter 2 and Figure 11.1 serves to refresh your memory on this concept.

CWMS—THE MOST EFFECTIVE TOOL FOR ENABLING THE WORK MANAGEMENT PROCESS

In order to move from a reactive work environment, to a proactive, and then optimized work environment, it is absolutely necessary to have an enabling CWMS solution that has been successfully implemented throughout operations. The following are some of the key building blocks for effective work management using a CWMS.

(1) Develop and implement a quality preventive maintenance program. A quality PM program is the heart of effective work management. Maintenance and operations staff should work together to decide on the right PM jobs for the various assets. These PM should be set up in the CWMS (unless they were set up during the CWMS

161

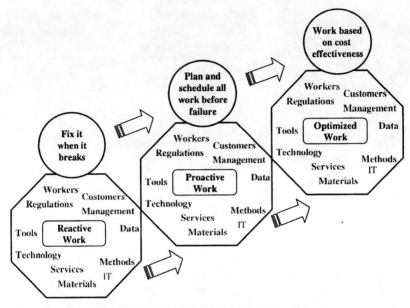

FIGURE 11.1 Work Management Practices.

implementation phase) with an appropriate triggering mechanism. This can be time-based (e.g., after a set number hours), calendar-based (e.g., monthly), seasonal (e.g., spring- and winter-related tasks), statistic-based (e.g., run hours from SCADA, mileage, gallons pumped) or a combination of these (e.g., do an overhaul each year or at 5000 run hours, whichever comes first). The actual jobs should be set up with appropriate tasks, resource assignments (by trade), materials and specifications/procedures. When these jobs are triggered (either automatically in the CWMS or manually by the planner/scheduler), PM WOs are created and are added to the WO backlog for scheduling.

(2) CWMS and total productive maintenance [clean, lubricate, adjust, inspect and repair (CLAIR)]. Total productive maintenance (TPM) is a best in class practice that promotes the combined concept of operations and maintenance work to take control of work, improve asset reliability and focus on high quality. Specifically, TPM recommends that operators be skilled up to do simple and routine maintenance tasks falling under the CLAIR (clean, lubricate, adjust, inspect and repair) category. This frees up the maintenance staff to do more core and complex jobs focused on improving asset

reliability and performance. Once the CLAIR jobs are identified, they should be set up in the CWMS as PMs or standard jobs (WOs created from them as needed) and standing work orders (time can be charged to these WOs for work where history is irrelevant). When these WOs are created for they are added to the WO backlog for planning and scheduling. Note that these jobs can be initiated as a work request in the case of minor repairs (usually of duration less than half an hour and requiring simple tools).

(3) The CWMS and a predictive maintenance program (PdM). Predictive maintenance (PdM), sometimes referred to as condition-based monitoring of assets, is simply a maintenance concept whose main objective is to track the health or deterioration rate of the asset. Effective PdM requires knowledge of the position of the asset on the deterioration curve at any point in time (with a great deal of confidence) and making corrective maintenance-type decisions just prior to failure. As you can see, this is a risky process and requires selecting appropriate predictive techniques for the asset in its unique operating environment, capturing quality data on a regular basis, trending and evaluating the data and making the call at the right time on a corrective maintenance job. When done right, PdM can help improve asset reliability, minimize maintenance costs (labor and materials), minimize opportunity costs due to assets being off the production or process line, and reduce or eliminate safety incidents (no more catastrophic failures with primary and secondary damage). There are many simple and sophisticated predictive techniques available today for any type of asset, these include: oil, vibration, infrared analysis; engine, pump, turbine analyzers, nondestructive testing techniques, smart pipeline "pigs" and closed circuit TV (CCTV) for pipe lines. The measurement task is usually set up as a PM in the CWMS to be triggered as a PM WO at the right frequency. The data is collected, trended and evaluated using specialized tools and software relevant to the technique and the corrective WRs are entered into the CWMS by the analyst. It is important that a PdM program is closely monitored for success, return on the investment and cost-effective asset reliability.

(4) Planning, scheduling and backlog management. Organizing the work in a manner so as to ensure a smooth flow as well as elimination of non-value-added steps is the key to effective planning and scheduling. Your organization may be fortunate to have employees who are solely responsible for planning and scheduling or this function may be carried out by individuals in addition to other duties.

Regardless of organizational structure, effective planning and scheduling are critical to taking control of work and moving to the ultimate vision of an optimized work environment. Work can either start off as a work request or go directly into the work order status if it is generated from a PM. This means that there are two backlogs to be managed: a WR backlog and a WO backlog.

- work request backlog—this is the responsibility of the planner. The work request backlog should not be more than a few days old. When planning is effective, WRs are usually approved by the right authority without delay and the planner can then create a simple WO in the planning status. A high WR backlog suggests problems with the approval process, an inefficient planning process or inadequate planning resources.
- work order backlog—this is the joint responsibility of the planner, scheduler and the crews or business units that are responsible for executing work. The work order backlog is usually a listing of work orders in the planning phase and active work orders that have been planned in detail and are awaiting the availability of manpower, tools and equipment, materials or access to the asset to perform work. When these four elements are in place, the WO can be scheduled with the certainty that it has the best chance of being done on time, schedule and budget. If any one of these elements is not in place [this can be as simple as a special bolt or gasket (may be small dollar value)] the asset cannot be commissioned and returned to service. A growing work order backlog suggests problems in assessing jobs, the planning process, scheduling issues (manpower, tools and equipment and material availability), the execution process, ability to take the asset out of service to work on it or too much unnecessary work.

(5) The CWMS and reliability centered maintenance (RCM). In sections 1 to 4 above, there has been a lot of reference to the development of reactive WOs, PM, standard jobs, predictive PM and corrective WOs. You are probably wondering how to decide on the right mix of work for your assets. Traditionally, one goes by the knowledge of the most experienced staff, the manufacturer's guidelines or just simply "winging it." There has been a recent surge in interest in using RCM as a method to develop the right mix of tactics for a company's assets. RCM is a scientific technique that helps to decide on the right maintenance mix of reactive, proactive and predictive maintenance for critical assets. RCM was first devel-

oped in the military as an approach to maintenance that provided a real guarantee of reliability of military equipment. This technique was later successfully adopted in the aircraft industry and has made a positive impact on reliability of commercial aircrafts. RCM is a step-by-step process that looks at every function of an asset, the possible failures (inability to carry out the function), the consequences of each failure and the failure mode. A logic tree is then used to determine the best way to deal with the failure—run to failure, redesign, and time-based or condition-based maintenance. Maintenance programs can be developed for each asset after exhausting all the possible ways an asset can fail. These programs are then duplicated in the CWMS in the form of PM or standard jobs. It is obvious that this can be a very long and tedious process; as a result RCM is usually reserved for critical assets or assets that have major performance issues in your operation.

THE CWMS AND BUDGETING

The hierarchy of performance centers that is developed in the CWMS during implementation serves a twofold purpose: it captures work and cost history at the asset level and rolls up costs at all other levels right up to the highest or company level. Cost can be captured in the categories of estimated, committed (or accrued) and actual. The CWMS also provides for a category of cost, called budgeted. In fact, if you have been using your CWMS for some time and your data is accurate it is possible to use the actual costs over the last year as a basis to develop a zero-based budget for the various performance centers (e.g., at the division and department levels). These budgets, when approved, can be used to determine the availability of funds during the course of the work management process. Some companies build interfaces to their financial system to ensure that any modifications to budgets are automatically updated in the CWMS at the performance center level. This means that each performance center must have a unique general ledger number for the interface to work. People who are required to manage budgets as part of their performance center can then easily use the CMWS to keep track of labor costs (internal and external), materials and services for operating budgets. If the CWMS has a capital projects module, then a similar approach can be used to manage capital budgets.

THE CWMS AND PERFORMANCE MANAGEMENT

During the course of doing work a significant amount of data is collected at the various performance centers in the hierarchy. This data is available in a year-to-date form or over any specified time period. It can be made available as computations done directly in the CWMS and presented on the various screens (we already talked about the various forms in which cost could be reported) or can be accessed through a report writer. These can be made available in the CWMS or can be exported to spreadsheets or other databases for manipulations, calculations and trending to aid decision support. The following are some of the performance data that can be obtained from a CWMS.

- work management
  —WR and WO backlogs
  —PM compliance
  —schedule compliance
  —ratio of reactive to proactive work
  —percentage of CLAIR work done by operators
  —number of safety work orders
- performance center
  —budgeted costs
  —estimated costs
  —committed or accrued costs
  —actual costs
- asset level
  —failure mode
  —reliability [mean time between failure (MTBF)]
  —mean time to repair (MTTR)
  —all the cost types discussed in performance center, above
  —total asset value (book, replacement)
  —active or inactive assets
  —asset condition (deterioration curve)
- inventory (can be by ABC classification)
  —inventory value
  —stores service level; number of stock outs
  —inventory turns
  —number of stock items
  —inventory shrinkage
  —slow moving items
  —obsolete items
  —number of items added to the stock over a specified time period
  —number of items removed from the stock over a specified time period
  —vendor performance data (captured at receiving)

- purchasing
  - —number of PRs and POs
  - —number of request for quotations
  - —number of contracts (blanket orders)
  - —cost per purchase order
- data for overall performance
  - —total cost per unit of product
  - —overtime costs
  - —maintenance cost as a percentage of total cost
  - —average number of CWMS systems users by performance center

Note that this list is not comprehensive, but rather provides some of the more popular measures used by various companies.

USING THE CWMS TO IMPROVE ASSET RELIABILITY

The CWMS captures and stores a wealth of asset-related information during the course of doing work. A CWMS can be used to support the asset management shift in behavior from risk avoidance to risk management if the right asset-related data is collected and used on a regular basis. Very few companies effectively use this data to improve asset reliability. The goal for every company that has invested in a CWMS is to leverage this unique tool to develop and sustain a behavior of continuous improvement. The cost and work history data that is captured at the asset level is a valuable indicator for asset performance problems. Continuous improvement starts with the planner when a WR shows up in his or her inbox for a particular asset. Instead of jumping into the planning activity, the planner should review the work history and identify the pattern of failure and the reasons for failure. It may be surprising to find out what this simple exercise can yield and the difference in the WO that emanates from the planning process.

The following example would serve to illustrate the point. A WR for a broken pump coupling comes in and the planner quickly turns it into a WO to replace the coupling. When good continuous improvement concepts are being followed, the planner checks the work history for the asset and sees that there has been three similar failures in the last six months; also, a quick look at similar pumps shows that there have been no failures like this in the last two years. A good planner will quickly figure out that replacing the coupling is really a band-aid solution and will see that they need to get at the root of the problem. A well thought out work order would include vibration analysis and laser alignment tasks to evaluate if there is a misalignment or unbalance problem that needs to be corrected. The asset would be placed under closer scrutiny and if there is a further failure then a more detailed investigation should be done; this could yield, for example, a change in coupling type or redesign of the drive system. The ultimate effect is improved asset reliability, reduced maintenance costs and, of course, a happier operator! Another key area for improving asset reliability is through condition-based monitoring where key parameters on the "health" of the asset are monitored and trended, and corrective WOs executed prior to failure.

A CWMS AND ASSET MANAGEMENT

The CWMS can be an important source of asset performance data when new assets are being designed to meet changing needs. As operators, maintainers get involved in the asset management process; they can rely on this information to provide valuable feedback and input into proposed designs and asset specifications. During the asset creation and commissioning phase of the asset life cycle, all the necessary asset-related information required for effective operations and maintenance can be specified and be entered into the system before the asset is made active. The commissioning data provides a valuable baseline "footprint" of information for condition monitoring in the future. Warranty and guarantee information will ensure getting value out of contractors and vendors and personnel do not spend critical resources on work that the vendor should be doing.

During the O&M phase of the asset life cycle, one can continuously track the condition of the asset and monitor its position on the deterioration curve. This data can be used to identify the work needed to bring the asset up to its original working condition. This analysis across all the assets in operations will provide the input for capital programs and a focus on the right priorities. In addition, problem assets (high failure rates) can be identified as formal CI projects where operators, maintainers and engineers come together to make recommendations on modifying, upgrading or replacing the asset.

A CWMS SUPPORTS SUCCESSION PLANNING AND CORPORATE KNOWLEDGE RETENTION

Many companies are struggling with the retirement of the baby boom-ers and are worried about being able to sustain their operations when their experienced employees move on. Many companies are reactive in dealing with succession planning challenge and find themselves frantically trying to fill positions internally with inexperienced and unskilled staff. In many cases they are also unable to find suitable candidates who can quickly get up to speed on their operations. A successful CWMS business solution can provide a pleasant solution to this challenge. A number of companies have found a bonus from their CWMS implementation in that all their key business processes are detailed in the CWMS with all the necessary specifications, procedures and work history. Once potential retirees are identified and a succession plan is developed, the CWMS can be a key tool for skills development and learning about the company business.

When experienced employees move on, they usually leave with a lot of empirical knowledge in their heads. If good work, operations and asset management practices are employed with the CWMS then a company can be assured that the key corporate knowledge areas will be protected, captured electronically and preserved for the future. In using the CWMS to support succession planning and corporate knowledge retention, the following areas should be given top priority.

- succession planning
    —customized end-user training documentation on the work and materials management process
    —tutorials that can provide a step-by-step training guide on the various phases of the work order and materials management process
    —customized reports used to support work and materials management
    —customized end-user training documentation on the safety and the permitting process (hot work, confined space, excavation, material safety data sheet, safety procedures)
- knowledge retention
    —quality PM program (with detailed PM by asset type)
    —work procedures for the various asset types (standard jobs)
    —bill of materials for the each asset
    —quality of work history with "reason for failure" that truly reflects why the asset failed
    —accurate asset information on the asset record
    —documented continuous improvement initiatives linked to the asset being investigated
    —updated drawings and procedures linked to the asset record

—documented predictive maintenance program
—documented reliability centered maintenance evaluations with all relevant details linked to the asset record
—documentation on the CWMS system configuration and the interface specifications and definition

CHAPTER 12

Keeping Current on the CWMS Solution

The pace of change with technology has been one of the most difficult challenges for many companies who have invested significant funds in a CWMS and an integrated technology solution. The following areas of change can work together to make the CWMS solution outdated within a very short period of time.

(1) Continued development and use of the internet as a means of delivering business solutions
(2) Continued research and development of the CWMS by the vendor
(3) Advances in software programming languages
(4) Continued research and development of the CWMS by the vendor
(5) Continued research and development of the operating system or database by the respective vendor
(6) Vendor discontinuation due to bankruptcy or acquisition by another company

The above list of changes all seem to be out of your control and it may seem futile to make any effort to stay current with your CWMS solution. In fact, many who have given up trying to keep current with their CWMS have found out, to their detriment, that the vendor no longer supports the old version of the software. Upgrading to the latest version is actually a completely new implementation with the associated high investment dollars and pain. What can a company do about this seemingly difficult challenge? There is a key concept that should be applied with respect to the use of a CWMS and a number of recommended steps that should be implemented.

"IT'S THE PRACTICES THAT ARE IMPORTANT—
NOT THE TECHNOLOGY"

A company should make every effort during the CWMS implementation and support phase to get end users to view the CWMS as another software tool to support their business practices. In this regard, *if you have solid work, operations and asset management processes that are well defined, documented and understood by all*, then changes in the CWMS and its components will be taken in stride with minimal impact on the users. An example in a very simple form is the practice of typing or report preparation. Once this skill is mastered, one can use MS Word, WordPerfect or any other word processing software to prepare a letter or report; being easily able to find the right functions or editing tools to quickly become proficient in report preparations on the new software. Similarly, if end users understand and master the practice of work management, then they will be easily able to create WRs, WOs or PM on a new version of the CWMS or on a completely new CWMS. In addition, focus should be *on ensuring that all records are fully defined (e.g., the asset record), all data captured during the work management process is of high quality and integrity and all configuration is properly documented.* When this is in place, a company is then able to easily move up to a new version of the CWMS or, in the worst case, a completely new CWMS, by exporting the existing data to the new system.

SOFTWARE DEVELOPMENT

In Chapter 6, we discussed how a system development life cycle approach could be used to include the CWMS in the overall integrated technology solution (Figure 12.1). This approach allows a company to be proactive in applying new releases and updating various business applications, database and operating systems in manageable chunks. In addition, significant internal changes to the CWMS configuration can be included in one of the step changes in a particular release. In Chapter 6, we introduced the idea of a working committee to proactively manage the changes that affect the integrated CWMS solution. This committee should be charged with developing a clear team charter with its vision and mission focused on development and implementation of plans to always have a current integrated technology solution and minimize the risk to the company's business due to external technology factors.

Managing software in this manner gives a company the insurance and peace of mind that their critical business operations can survive the de-

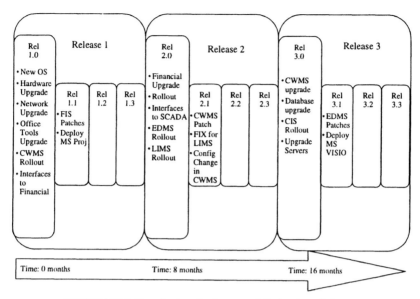

FIGURE 12.1 *Developing the Integrated Technology Solution.*

mise of one of their business software vendors. This approach, however, does not enable early detection of signs of distress in the vendor's operations, thereby taking appropriate action. In addition, this makes a company very reactive and unable to influence the process for updates and new releases of the CWMS (and other software) from the vendor. Getting actively involved in the vendor's user group and their annual conference will help a company deal with these problems.

VENDOR SUPPORT

During the CWMS selection process, a key parameter in evaluating potential CWMS vendor's ability to meet your business partnership would be their user support mechanisms. Theses fall into three main areas: software and technical support, user groups and user conferences.

Software and Technical Support

This area is covered by the maintenance agreement determined at the contract negotiation phase of the selection process. It covers areas such as

- resolution of software "bugs" or conflicts in the program
- configuration problems or challenges
- resolution of system performance issues
- help in taking advantage of error corrections (ECs), software patches, new releases, etc.

Vendors are able to be effective in this area through the use of help lines, issue-tracking software, vendor training programs and a comprehensive website.

User Group

A user group is one of the key ways the vendor keeps the user community energized; they also use this avenue as a way to identify development needs for the CWMS. Your company can benefit from becoming part of the user group by learning from the experiences of other users in terms of work practices, unique configuration designs (to deal with problems) and special reports. In addition, if there are special business needs that your CWMS does not currently support, you can lobby (through the user group) for the vendor to include this into their development items for the next release. There is also the added bonus of keeping abreast of the health of the vendor's organization and being able to provide advance warning to the IT committee of potential vendor problems.

The User Conference

Most reputable vendors hold an annual user conference that provides a forum for clients to showcase unique successes they have had with the CWMS, new developments from the vendor's research and development group and inspirational presentations from industry experts. Of course, the user conference provides an opportunity for networking and having a good time!

BENCHMARKING PERFORMANCE

In Chapter 11 we discussed key performance metrics related to a successful CWMS implementation. An evaluation of the impact on business performance will give a clear indication of the benefits from the CWMS. A company should continuously be benchmarking performance (technology-specific and business-related) with other user group members to ensure they are getting the most of their system, at least when compared to similar industries. In addition, they should always be scanning the industry environment as part of the strategic planning process. This should help identify what practices the company is good at, what practices are important, but need more work to be beneficial and what practices are not yet on the radar, but need to be adopted in order to stay competitive. It will be found that, in general, the CWMS is a key enabling solution for getting and sustaining competitiveness.

CHAPTER 13

Why Do CWMS Fail? Pitfalls and Solutions

Every business that uses assets to provide a service or create a product can benefit tremendously from enabling their work management process with a CWMS. Many companies have recognized this opportunity and have initiated projects to select and implement this type of technology. The results have been depressing—many surveys have shown that over 50% of CWMS implementations are failures. Companies usually recognize this after many years of implementation and after investing many millions of dollars and precious labor resources. In addition, of the 50% that have shown some signs of success, many are yet to realize the full potential from a CWMS. You are probably wondering if it is worth even thinking about a CWMS. If you already have a CWMS and are struggling with the implementation, you must be wondering if you should throw in the towel and call the project off. The past twelve chapters of this book have provided sensible advice on the selection and implementation process for a CWMS. Indeed, the concepts and methodologies can be applied to any major software project. This chapter will provide the major reasons for CWMS failures and some practical advice to help avoid or recover from these problems.

TYPICAL PITFALLS IN CWMS PROJECTS AND RECOMMENDATIONS ON HOW TO AVOID THEM

(1) Being unable to justify the investment. Many CWMS projects don't ever get off the ground because of the inability of managers to convince the accountants of the returns on a CWMS invest-

ment. Most supervisors and managers recognize the need for a CWMS and understand how the CWMS can have a positive impact on taking control of work. In fact, a good suggestion to managers is that using a CWMS to support work management is similar to having office productivity tools to support your business. It is absolutely necessary to achieve and sustain competitiveness. However, budget submissions are usually rejected for a number of reasons. These include inadequate research into cost of selecting and implementing the system and very little quantification of benefits. In a number of cases, the budget submission is not accompanied by a business case and the rationale for a CWMS is weak. It is obvious that the only outcome of these requests would be negative, given the number of competing projects for the limited annual investment budget. In Chapter 3, we discussed how you can develop an invincible business case that not only helps win approval for scarce dollars but also creates the road map for benefits tracking as the project unfolds.

(2) Flavor of the day—getting caught up with the "bells and whistles." CWMS vendors are very good at marketing their products and tend to showcase their solutions where decision makers will take notice. These companies have display booths at major operations and maintenance conferences (e.g., WEFTEC), advertise in trade journals and the Internet and direct market to selected companies. Sometimes decision makers get the CWMS bug and decide that their company must have a CWMS and even decide to buy a particular product that they saw based on their impression of the salesperson. The end result is a vendor and software solution being forced upon people who may not be pleased with the particular CWMS selected. Implementation then drags on, no one buys in and the senior executive loses interest, turning attention to other projects. The CWMS then becomes a chore for users who see it as extra work and no benefit to them or the company. Work and cost history tend to be poor quality and are rarely used for continuous improvement.

(3) Being forced to use a CWMS as part of an ERP solution. A common problem that many operations and maintenance professionals face when trying to procure a CWMS is being forced to use the CWMS module supplied with the overall enterprise resource planning (ERP) business software that the company uses for its administration and production operations. Many ERP vendors have recognized the growing trends in the lucrative CWMS mar-

ket and have decided to capitalize on them. Over the last five years, they have all developed their work management modules in the hope of attracting clients who are fearful of high interface development and maintenance costs. In many cases, the CWMS is not their core business and the functionality does not compare favorably with CWMS vendors who are focused soley on the CWMS market. An end result, as in (2) above, is the most likely outcome for most CWMS solutions that are an afterthought from ERP solutions.

(4) Going it alone. Many companies (in an effort to reduce costs) decide to select and implement a CWMS without any expert help. Some have been successful, but most have experienced great difficulty defining their requirements, evaluating the various products and vendors in the market, negotiating a mutually beneficial contract and implementing the system in a timely manner. Besides taking an unduly long time, there is a tendency to configure the system to do what has been done for years. Their work practices may be efficient in some instances, but in many cases, they tend to be highly reactive. It is necessary to balance the benefits from hiring a CWMS expert with the benefits from a timely and successful implementation.

(5) Realizing that the product does not match the business need. In the RFP process, the product demonstration phase is where the vendor gets an opportunity to showcase their company and product. You also get an opportunity to evaluate how well the vendor matches your business partnership requirements and how well the product meets your functional requirements. A slick salesman can easily convince a company that the software is capable of doing everything possible. It is not uncommon to find out, after a decision has been made to select a particular vendor and solution, that you have bought "vaporware"—software that is being developed or functionality that is not available. This situation is exacerbated when the evaluation process and criteria are very loose. It then finds it difficult to make a rational decision and selection team members tend to go with "gut feel"—in this case, the vendor that made the biggest impression on them. A company could also be exposed to possible litigation from other candidates who think (and rightly so) that the selection process was not fair.

(6) Finding the cheapest solution. A similar issue to (5) above is the pressure (by corporate finance or purchasing) to go with the cheapest bid. In doing this a company might have to accept less

functionality and settle for poor response to system maintenance issues and new releases. The cheapest solution could also could compromise the work management process or force giving up valuable functionality in the current manual or electronic system. This could cause some lack of buy-in for the system and easily result in the CWMS becoming an ineffective tool.

(7) Finding that the vendor does not meet partnership expectations. Many companies have selected software vendors to partner with them and create a CWMS solution, only to find out that the vendor was only interested in the sale. They are then left with little support for implementation, poor response to system maintenance issues, no regular research and development (reflected in regular new releases) and dull or nonexistent client-user network and annual conferences. Vendors with this type of performance are prime candidates for takeover, acquisition or bankruptcy. When this happens a company is left with a business application that they are not adequately prepared to support and certainly in no position to upgrade to meet technological advances. The only insurance, in this situation, is to have a copy of the software code in escrow allowing the IT staff to keep the CWMS ticking along, thus buying enough time to upgrade to a new product and vendor.

(8) Believing that the CWMS is an IT project. A very common reason for CWMS failure is the perception that this is another information technology (IT) project dreamt up by the IT department. The IT department, with good intentions, understands the importance of a CWMS and goes about selecting and implementing the system with little or no involvement of the operations and maintenance staff. The configured tool is generally not reflective of the needs of the end users, has very impractical user setups and generally results in a system that is used only because the end users are instructed to use it.

(9) Having too much end user involvement—paralysis by analysis. Even if a company is careful to avoid the above pitfalls and tries to use expert help and involves staff as much as possible, they have to guard against the "paralysis by analysis" syndrome. In this situation, too much analysis is being done at the selection and implementation stage in order to get the perfect solution. This results in an inordinate amount of time being spent on these phases with high consulting costs and overtime to replace team members in the workplace. The CWMS project drags on (it seems like forever for many anxious end users) and management may even contemplate

canceling the project and regarding the investment to date as a sunk cost. Careful selection of CWMS expert help, your team members and limiting the team size to a small and manageable number are key suggestions to help with this problem. Remember, you can always make changes to the system after going live—you do not have to get everything right to start seeing benefits from the implementation.

(10) Having too little end user involvement. A company should have to be careful about having too little end-user involvement in the selection and implementation process. In this case, there is risk of losing valuable input on the critical needs of the business as well as lack of buy-in for the system when it goes live.

(11) Having users feel threatened by the CWMS. Many users (especially older users or those who are not computer literate) are fearful of the computer and see the CWMS as a technology that would make their jobs redundant when it is implemented. Similarly, end users may see the CWMS as a tool that can be used to track every single minute of their workday and may feel anxious and angry about the implementation. In some extreme cases, employees have been known to sabotage the system, put in poor data or steal computers so that they don't have to use the system. A well-executed communication plan, designed to get the right message to the various stakeholders at the right time, would go a long way to allay these fears and help employees understand the benefits to themselves as well as the company.

(12) Having poor networking with fellow users. Many companies invest millions of dollars in a CWMS using a capital budget and then make it extremely difficult to get additional funds for maintaining and continuously improving the integrated solution. Two areas that are often overlooked are involvement in the vendor's user group and attendance at the annual conference. Usually the investment in this area is insignificant in terms of time and dollars; however, the returns from networking with people who have learned how to resolve work practice issues using the CWMS as well as software-related issues is tremendous. In addition, the annual conference is a great opportunity to showcase your company and the good work you have done using the CWMS. Instead of thinking that sending employees to the conference is a perk and they will be having a good time, it should be considered as valued training, preparing your company for new software developments and advances in technology. It should be used as a forum for developing

potential leaders in the company. Finally, the vendors use the annual conference and other user-group activities to seek input from users in order to set the direction for their research and development group. This is a great opportunity for your company to make recommendations for functionality or user friendliness improvements that would make the work management practice more effective.

(13) Having poor life cycle management. The CWMS is an intangible (or virtual) asset into which a company has invested a lot of time and money. In order to maximize the returns from this investment it is important to understand the CWMS life cycle and apply appropriate asset management techniques to each phase. The CWMS, after it is configured and implemented, is probably one of the most critical assets in your company because the entire business is now supported by the CWMS. Many companies do not think of the CWMS as an asset and they miss many opportunities to maximize the returns for this important investment. The following discussion around the life cycle of a CWMS will provide some guidance on doing the right things at the right time.

- Identify and design needs—Accurate identification of your requirements is important to selection and implementation of the best CWMS solution for your company. Mistakes at this stage will set down a specific direction and you may only realize the downside after the software is implemented. Involvement of the right people and understanding best in class work, operations and asset management practices is key to success in this phase.
- Procure/implement—We discussed the process of selecting the best solution to support your business in earlier chapters of this book. Inadequate attention to this phase could result in a poor software solution and/or a vendor who does not meet your business partnership expectations for the life of the software. It is important to follow the recommendations on selection and implementation provided in this book in order to avoid these problems.
- Operate, maintain, upgrade or modify—This phase refers to getting the most out of your CWMS in using it to support your business practices. If you employ all of the techniques learned so far, you will find that the CWMS is a great tool that provides significant benefit to operations and maintenance and, indeed, to a number of other groups such as

finance, materials management and engineering. If you also employ the concepts discussed on staying current on your CWMS solution, you will be able to maintain the system on a regular basis by making careful modifications that don't compromise the ability to take advantage of the vendor upgrades and new releases.

- Replace—As with any asset, there must be replacement of the asset at the end of its life cycle. Many companies are so out of touch with their CWMS they don't even recognize that they are at this phase of the life cycle and keep on using a system that is not effective and is high in upkeep costs. The CWMS can be at the end of its life cycle because of obsolescence due to advances in technology (e.g., mainframe systems), the vendor going out of business or being acquired by the competitor who does not plan to support your solution or radical changes in your business and the CWMS is now obsolete or ineffective. Again, staying current with your system, being aware of the development in technology and always viewing the CWMS as asset that provides a return on investment are some good ways to act decisively in making a replacement decision. A sound business case is usually a key requirement at this stage. (Note: the CWMS as an important asset requiring effective asset management will be discussed in some more detail in Chapter 14.)

(14) Having no benefits tracking. It is important that we know how to track any benefits derived from the CWMS solution if making an attractive return on investment was one of the selling points for the project. If a good business case is made at the start of the CWMS project, defining costs and benefits in detail, then it is very easy to use the business case spreadsheet to do benefits tracking over the life of the project. Project sponsors should continue to show interest in the CWMS after implementation and ask for evidence supporting the benefits. When benefits are not in line with what was projected, then the sponsors should identify the causes and take the necessary action to have them corrected as soon as possible.

CHAPTER 14

Future Trends in the CWMS Industry

Computerized work management systems will always be around, but in the future, they will be very different from what we are used to today. Rapid advances and breakthroughs in technology, changes in work practices and work environment, design of the various asset types and market forces will drive the changes in the CWMS.

TECHNOLOGY CHANGES

There are number of trends in the technology sector that will influence the development of the CWMS technology.

(1) Rapid increase in computing power (CPU processing speed) as defined by Moore's law. As computers become faster and are able to process more complex algorithms, so too, will CWMS software become more complex, not only doing basic functions but also performing complex computations.

(2) Cheap and large volumes of storage space will allow the capture and storage of much more data than what is possible today.

(3) Miniaturization of hardware will result in complete CWMS modules operating on hand-held devices, allowing realistic use of the CWMS to support field staff. Continued developments in computer hardware that fits into headsets will allow delivery of CWMS-related information (possibly all the CWMS modules), allowing the worker to have both hands free and, at the same time, access vital information needed to troubleshoot and repair the asset.

185

(4) Improvements in wireless technology will allow the hand-held devices to communicate with main servers as well as microprocessors in critical assets.

(5) Voice recognition will also influence how end-users interact with the CWMS. Vendors will actively pursue this technology in order to minimize the age-old problem of end users' unwillingness to use the keyboard for data entry.

(6) The Internet will continue to revolutionize how software is deployed and accessed and at the same time provide key links to other valuable information sites necessary to support effective work management. The Internet will also be the method of choice for delivering software and upgrades from the vendor (instead of the shipment of CDs as happens today).

(7) Standardization of programming languages and software design guidelines will eventually force CWMS vendors to adopt the same approach to design of their products. This will drive vendors to differentiate their product by adding more complex functionality, improving service levels and offering attractive prices just to get new customers. The clients will benefit in the long run because standardization will allow them to easily replace their CWMS if the vendor goes out of business or if they have a pressing business need to move to another system.

PRACTICES-RELATED CHANGES

More and more companies are identifying best practices in asset and operations management as well as work management as a main source of competitiveness and sustainability for their company. The current battle between CWMS "best of breed" solutions and the CWMS module being part of an enterprise resource planning software will be a redundant discussion as vendors start developing a hybrid system that seeks to provide solutions to all three practice areas (work, asset and operations management). In addition, CWMS vendors will provide "decision support" modules as a standard offering as more companies adopt performance management to achieve and sustain competitiveness. In the future, clients will have one-stop shopping for most of the functionality not typically provided by the ERP systems.

In addition, ongoing improvements in asset design (discussed in the next paragraph) will result in more durable materials that will reduce or eliminate the effect of abrasion, corrosion and erosion. Materials will be of lighter weight, will be much stronger and will be able to withstand higher stresses. The net result will be slower natural deterioration rates and lower incidences of failures due to overloading. Maintenance practices will move from proactive to the optimized realm, where most of the work done on assets will be predictive in nature (over 60% of PMs), with a focus on knowing the location of each asset on its deterioration curve at any point in time.

ASSET DESIGN

There will be an increased sophistication in asset design with a trend to smart control systems. We will see most high cost and critical assets being equipped with CPUs that allow these assets to track their overall "health" and also perform self-diagnostics. In this way, the asset can continuously track and trend relevant data. A mini version of the CWMS can reside on this CPU and would facilitate the basic work management process. In the event of major deviations from targets or set points the asset will

- initiate corrective action if the problem is due to changes in operating parameters, or initiate a work request for operations attention
- initiate a suitable work request if the problem is one that needs maintenance attention

These work requests can be sent in the appropriate format to the main CWMS system, stored in memory for downloading to a PDA or printed out at the closest printer location. The CPU will also have a record of the active PM and would also be able to trigger any PM that is due on the asset within set time frames. In the future, a worker assigned to take care of a particular group of assets would be able to enter a particular building or work area and all assets would communicate wirelessly with the worker's PDA and download any needed work or information. When work is completed, all data entered by the worker will be immediately uploaded to the asset's CPU and its database updated (at the same time resetting parameters, e.g., PM). This database could be part of an overall network of databases that is tied to the main CWMS servers.

There will be a major drive toward modular components that will be replaced instead of taking additional valuable time for repairs. In addition to extended mean time between failures (MTBF), there will be vast improvements in mean time to repair (MTTR). As indicated in the previous paragraph, asset design will also focus on improved durability, reliability and reduced weight. Advances in nanotechnology will drive these changes and open up many more exciting opportunities in asset design.

PEOPLE-RELATED CHANGES

There are many future people-related changes that will impact how the CWMS is designed and how it will operate. The most significant will be computer literacy. As the current generation grows up with technology and computers as a part of daily life, employees will be able to easily deal with more complex software screens. The CWMS industry will be able to add more functionality to enable optimized work, asset management and performance management without surpassing the user's capability to easily use these functionalities (as happens now). The focus on balanced life styles will see a reduction in the work hours and consequently less and less time on-site and around the assets. Consequently, there will be an increased dependency on off-shift and off-hours support for the operations. The CWMS will step in to fill this need through wireless communication of alarms, faults and any other critical problems to the standby or responsible personnel. Seamless integration with process control and SCADA will provide a remote first line of defense. If it is necessary to make a visit to the asset, the CWMS will enable the worker to properly plan the work so that on-site time and asset down time is reduced to a minimum.

INDUSTRY TEMPLATING

Unrelenting competition in the CWMS market has forced many vendors to differentiate their products and company. You can find vendors selling their systems as enterprise asset management systems (EAMS), computerized maintenance management systems (CMMS), computerized work management systems (CWMS) or total maintenance solutions (TMS). They all provide base functionality to support the work management process with some differentiation in minor areas. As the market matures, vendors will focus on ease and timeliness of implementation, together with a promise to help future clients with knowledge from previous or existing client experiences. One area of differentiation would be to sell preconfigured systems (based on industries best practices and their positive experiences with similar clients) unique to the industry segment. A company would be able to purchase a CWMS already configured (75%–80%) to meet the water, wastewater, public works, electric, gas, pharmaceutical, food, process mining industries. Some minor configuration to set up users and simulate company policies (e.g., approval routes and limits) would be necessary to get the system ready for use. The time and cost to implement will be significantly reduced; however, a company may not be able to conduct some their unique business needs on the system. This trend of industry templating will gain momentum but will be available only through the big players because the cost to the vendor to keep current with best practices would be high.

APPLICATION SERVICE PROVIDERS (ASPs)

The ASP (vendor) will provide configured software, store all CWMS-related database records on their server farms and charge a monthly fee for use of the system. The software is made available to end-users through a secured Internet. In this way a company does not have to be concerned about software maintenance, system upgrades and servers. Some vendors have been experimenting with the ASP concept but have had limited success so far. Companies are still uncomfortable having all of their critical information stored and managed by a third party. In addition, the ASP concept is a bit more complex to manage if a company has incorporated the CWMS into an integrated technology solution. The ASP concept could be feasible for small companies with limited staffing resources.

CONSOLIDATION OF THE MARKET PLAYERS
TO PROVIDE A SEAMLESSLY INTEGRATED
BUSINESS TOOL

The CWMS market is continually changing with many new companies and products becoming available each a year and many existing players going out of business or being acquired. Some of these decisions are strategic because of a need to fill niche requirements, acquire a new product line (without spending the time and money to develop it) or eliminate the competition and gain their clients. In the future, the big software vendors will focus on developing complete business solutions. The ERP vendors will continue to build up their work management functionality and reputation in this area. Similarly, the traditional CWMS vendors will continue to encroach on the ERP market segment—refining their materials management, financial and human resources offerings. Vendors will merge or be acquired to provide a complete solution for specific industry segments. The recent move by Microsoft to get into the work management industry and the small business software market is an indication of things to come. As discussed in Chapter 13, these changes will leave the unprepared in very vulnerable situations.

CONCLUSION

This book has provided a step-by-step guide to the CWMS world by making some sense out of the complex and sometimes intimidating activities required to select, implement and effectively use a CWMS to facilitate a company's business needs. The CWMS can be viewed as another asset (in fact it would be many times costlier than most existing assets) and should be managed around the asset life cycle in a similar fashion.

- Needs identification—required to improve productivity, cost effectively manage the work process and asset management and support corporate knowledge retention. The CWMS is a "must have" software if you plan to be competitive in business and sustain competitiveness.
- Plan and evaluate—like any other critical asset, good planning and evaluation are important for this major investment. This requires careful understanding of a company's needs, involvement of all key players, development of a business case and selling the program to executive sponsors.
- Design—this phase requires a full understanding of what is required of the software (functional requirements), how it fits into your current hardware and software technology environment (technical requirements) and how it supports your physical work environment (fixed and/or mobile access). In addition, it is essential to define what is expected from the business partnership with the potential CWMS vendor over the life of this important asset.
- Purchase/create/implement—a solid selection and implementation process is critical to identifying the vendor and product that best meets your business needs. Again, as in the case of a physical asset, all the key players must work together for a good selection decision. Similarly, the appropriate involvement of personnel (end users and support groups) with the right mix of consulting and vendor support is also key to a successful implementation.
- Commissioning—as with commission of any major asset, good

planning and "go live" preparation are critical to success. Rigorous system testing in the implementation phase, effective and timely training of end users, detailed check sheets and checks, a good support system (help desk) and a good communication plan for going live are necessary to make it through this major milestone with minimal problems. The decision to run an old system in parallel for some time or shut down and start using the new system immediately would be one of the major decisions at this stage.

- Operate and maintain—operating and maintaining the CWMS should be given the same level of importance and attention as would be given to a critical physical asset. You need to ensure that the asset is used properly in support of your business practices with the desired return on investment identified at the "planning and evaluation" phase. You need to work closely with the vendor to ensure that systems issues are addressed promptly with little impact on end users. Minor system upgrades or patches should be done transparently to the end users. The goal is ensure that practices are properly set up in the CWMS, that end users see the system as an enabling tool and all that data is of high quality and integrity. This approach to using the CWMS pays big dividends at the replacment phase of the life cycle.
- Modify or upgrade—if you are doing a good job of keeping track of the asset's ability to meet your business needs, you would always know if you were current on your system. The decision to upgrade to another release or make some programming changes (or add interfaces to other business systems) should be based on sound rationale and should be planned and implemented using the system development life cycle approach. (Note that this approach should also be employed for making major configuration changes and applying patches to the system.)
- Decommission—as in the case of any asset, there comes a time when the asset outlives its usefulness and must be replaced, in the case of a CWMS, it can be premature (because of market forces—mergers/acquisitions, vendor bankruptcy or obsolete technology). It is important to always scan the CWMS market and industry to be aware of these changes and be prepared for the day when you need to shut down and replace your CWMS. Regular attendance at conferences (vendor annual conferences, trades hows and specialty conferences) and involvement in the vendor user's group will give adequate warning of pending problems as well as awareness of any advances in CWMS technology.

- Replace—replacment of your CWMS should be given the same effort and attention as when you first selected and implemented your solution. You should have learned a number of important lessons that would make this time around much easier, less costly and a whole lot more fun.

Finally, by applying a bit of creativity and making some adjustments for unique business processes, you can easily apply the concepts and techniques discussed in this book to select and implement other major business applications.

Case Studies of CWMS Projects

1.1 Background on Company

Ideal City is major water, wastewater utility in North America and serves an average population of 2.2 million residents. In an effort to become competitive, provide value to its residents and keep the water and wastewater operations in the public domain, Ideal City embarked on an overall optimization program (with a supporting business case) using consulting expertise. The City's executive management team developed a vision for revised practices, supported by a team based organization and an integrated enabling technology solution. The City considered taking control of its work management practices as one of the most important roads on its journey to competitiveness and sustainability. The CWMS track of the program was conceived as the way to achieve the vision of program driven work.

1.2 Description of CWMS Project

The CWMS track had a mandate to select and implement a CWMS as part of an integrated technology solution needed to maintain the City's water and wastewater assets. The CWMS project track of the optimization program followed a standard approach for system selection and implementation as follows:

- City Selection Team supported by consulting expertise

- Definition of functional and technical requirements based on revised work and materials management processes
- Use of the RFI, RFP, Demo, Reference Checks and Contract negotiation process to select a vendor and product that best met their requirements for software and a business partnership.
- City Implementation Team supported by consulting resources
- Use of the conference room pilot (configuration, data collection/conversion, testing and training) followed by sequential rollout to the major treatment plants
- Development of appropriate interfaces to other key business applications (Process Control, and SCADA, Decision Support System, Financials) following a structured approach based on the SDLC process
- Transition of system ownership to the facilities and support to trained IT professionals

1.3 Results

The optimization program is close to the end of its 10 year project life (scheduled completion in 2004). As of the date of writing of this book the City has been and has able to make quantum leaps in improving its business operations, saving over $30M US on its annual budget and still continues to maintain a high level of service to its residents.

1.4 Opportunities

Ideal City is a solid example for water and wastewater utilities that are keen on achieving a culture of competitiveness and sustainability. Ideal City has found a way with its external partners to optimize the practices, organization and technology components of its business. It has made significant strides in using a CWMS to enable its work and materials management practices. The City needs to focus on moving to a culture of Optimized Work by introducing the right mix of reactive and proactive work through the use RCM and PdM techniques. The City also needs to develop its asset management practice with a goal of maximizing the investment the citizens have made in the asset infrastructure.

CASE STUDY # 2—PUBLIC WORKS

2.1 Background on Company

"See the Light" City is a typical small North American city struggling to maintain public works services with a dwindling population (and consequential reduced revenue base). The Public Works (PW) Department is responsible for operating and maintaining the City's roads, street lighting and signage, parks and open spaces, municipal buildings and airport, fleet and transit service. For many years the PW department has carried out its work management using a manual reactive process in many of its operating Sections. The practices were not standard and in some cases everything was verbal with no documentation. Some Sections such as its fleet operations had recently selected and implemented a Fleet Management System specifically designed and configured for managing a fleet type of business. The Fleet section was able to dramatically improve its service to its internal customers and was able to demonstrate fiscal responsibility in the way it conducted its business. This prompted the Director to initiate an improvement project aimed at better service at a lower cost. Selecting and implementing a department wide CWMS was considered to be a foundation piece on the journey to cost effectiveness.

2.2 Description of CWMS Project

The PW department formed a Steering Team to provide guidance and support for the project. The first task of the team was to hire consulting expertise to help them understand how a CWMS can improve their business and how it can be implemented successfully. A business case was developed together with a detailed project plan and a selection team was created with members of senior managers from each of the key business functions (including IT and Materials Management). The Selection Team is currently working with the consultant to find a suitable vendor and product (that best matches the PW department's business needs) to partner with on this important project.

2.3 Results

This project is still in its infancy, but has a very solid and realistic vision. The PW department has been able to complete a definition of its services, and some process improvement of its work management processes. This has allowed the selection team to develop functional requirements that would meet at least 90% of the functionality for work, capital projects and materials management for all of its sections. It was decided that any unique requirements such as Pavement Management Systems (unique to road construction maintenance would be interfaced to the CWMS. Employees however, have been against the CWMS project and are fearful that it would be used as a tool to monitor their performance. In addition, there are number of older employees who are not computer literate in the PW department.

2.4 Opportunities

The PW Department can get a larger return on its investment if it considers the CWMS to be a part of an integrated technology solution. It has to be careful to manage the change process carefully and avoid alienating its employees who consider the CWMS a threat to job security. They should add some frontline members to the implementation team. Regular honest and open communication together with focused training would go a long way in overcoming this hurdle.

CASE STUDY # 3—MINING

3.1 Background on Company

The XYZ Mining Company is based in North America and produces potash for use as fertilizer. XYZ continuously works the potash deposits 800 to 1000 feet underground and processes the raw extract into fertilizer grade product through its surface processing plant. Potash mining (as in the case with most mining operations) presents severe challenges to the maintenance department for taking care of asset operating continuously in a hot and a harsh environment. Suppressed market prices and unrelenting competition in the potash mining business made cost effective production a major strategic goal for XYZ mining. The maintenance department was given a mandate to increase asset availability and at the same time reduce the overall maintenance costs. The department's response to the challenge was to take a hard look at its maintenance and materials management practices and how they could leverage technology to become cost effective. The CWMS project was born as a direct result of these challenges.

3.2 Description of CWMS Project

The maintenance department conducted some preliminary research on the CWMS market and decided to select a suitable software using internal resources. A selection and implementation team was formed (led by a maintenance engineer) and they developed the functional requirements for the software based on minor improvements to the existing work and material management practices. The RFP, Demo and Reference check steps were employed to select a vendor and product. The vendor worked with the CWMS team conduct a conference room pilot (configuration, data conversion and collection, testing and training), development of interfaces to the financial system and roll out the software by modules—material management followed by work management. The vendor provided consulting expertise (maintenance consultant) to support the conference room pilot. The company's existing technology group provided support for the software.

3.3 Results

The team was able to successfully replace the old legacy (mainframe) system with the more modern CWMS. The materials management team was able to successfully leverage the CWMS to support the maintenance departments work activities. However, work practices had not changed significantly for the maintenance group and the large dollars in cost improvements were not achieved. Since no business case was developed for the project it has been difficult to quantify success and track it against original projections. The team has been slowly transitioning to a proactive work environment by using the CWMS to develop and implement a PM program and to practice effective planning and scheduling.

3.4 Opportunities

XYZ Mining has made an important step in replacing the old legacy mainframe system with a modern CWMS. There is a lot of work ahead to achieve the difficult goal of consistently high asset availability at a minimal cost. XYZ has to consider reengineering of its work processes, optimization of the PM program (ensure that the right PMs are in place through use of RCM and PdM) and moving to the appropriate mix of reactive and proactive work. XYZ should also embrace the SDLC concept and provide an enabling technology solution to support cost effective work and performance management. XYZ should also consider implementing an asset management practice and leverage the CWMS to maximize the reliability of all of its assets.

CASE STUDY # 4—PULP AND PAPER

4.1 Background on Company

The ABC Pulp and Paper Company is located in North America and is a major player in the hotly contested pulp and paper industry. The company has significant investment in assets in the logging, pulp and paper production processes. A large warehouse system manages both finished goods and MRO (Maintenance, Overhaul and Repairs) spares. ABC has long recognized the need to have a cost effective operations if it wants to complete the in the industry. Joe Bloggs, the VP of Operations and Maintenance have been on the defense lately and have been unable to explain the poor asset availability and high overtime in the operations. Joe has been frantically researching maintenance magazines and trade journals for answers. He has seen, in many of these publications, that the CWMS are the savior for people who find themselves in his position. Joe was able to convince his boss that he can turn things around if he got approval and funds to purchase and implement a CWMS. Joe got the necessary approval and a small budget ($100K). He immediately delegated full responsibility to his Chuck (the maintenance manager) for selecting and implementing the system. Joe even provided Chuck with copies of advertisements he had seen in the various magazines.

4.2 Description of CWMS Project

Chuck called up a few vendors and had them provide a demo in his office with his maintenance supervisors present. They were impressed by everything they saw and decided to go with the cheapest. The vendor reassured them that implementation was extremely easy and they would be able to be up and running in 3 months. He also committed to being on site at any time they needed help.

4.3 Results

As you would guess, this project turned out to be a dismal failure with finger pointing and assignment of blame being the only quantifiable results. The vendor provided no support, the software turned out to be incompatible with a number of the existing systems being used by the company, data collection was an enormous task, no improvements were made to the reactive maintenance process and there was no buy-in from any operations and frontline maintenance staff. To make matters worse, both Joe and Chuck found to, their horror, that the vendor had gone bankrupt and was not sure if his company was going to be around anymore.

4.4 Opportunities

After reading the A to Z of CWMS, I am sure you would be able to recommend to Joe (if he is still around) to consider hiring a reputable consultant to select and implement a CWMS. The consultant should help the team, develop proper needs for a CWMS supported by a business case, redesign its work and materials management processes and follow the recommended selection and implementation processes in this book.

Glossary of Terms

"As Is" work processes—documentation of the existing work processes in your operations as part of the reengineering process

Asset—entity that can be used to meet the needs of a client or customer by: performing an operation, functioning as part of a process, producing a product or performing a service

Asset Management—the optimization of the life cycle of an asset to meet performance standards in a safe and environmentally sound manner through smart: Planning, Investment, Financing, Engineering, Operations, Maintenance, Refurbishment and Replacement

BOM (Bill Of Materials)—listing of spare parts needed to maintain the asset

BOH (Balance On Hand)—quantity of stock item in the warehouse, this is a dynamic number and changes based on inventory transactions

CCTV—Closed Circuit Television, used to inspect sewer lines etc.

CLAIR—Cleaning, Lubricating, Adjustment, Inspection and Repair type work done by operators in a Total Productive Operations environment

CRP (Conference Room Pilot)—software implementation phase dedicated to training of the core team, loading of test data, configuration and testing of the system

CWMS (Computerized Work Management System)—software used to execute work management and related transactions and at the same time store data needed to support work and cost history

EAMS (Enterprise Asset Management System)—same definition as CWMS but with an additional focus on functionality aimed at asset condition tracking and extending asset reliability

EDMS (Electronic Document Management System)—software used to electronically store and manage documents in a secure environment

GIS—Geographical Information Systems (a computer business application that provides a view of assets based on maps)

Interface—software progras that link different business software allowing the timely exchange of information needed to support various business processes

JIT (Just In Time)—refers to materials management (inventory and purchasing) arrangements that ensures any materials or services are there just in time to support the work and operations processes (usually the responsibility for JIT is placed on the vendor with appropriate terms and conditions)

LAN (Local Area Network)—network infrastructure or servers, computers, terminals, interconnecting cables, printers and other peripheral devices local to a plant or facility

MRO Spares (Maintenance, Repairs and Overhaul Spares)—used in the support of the work management process (items usually stocked in the warehouse)

MSDS—Material Safety Data Sheet, provides key safety information on materials (stocked or direct purchase) for storage and handling

MTBF—Mean Time Between Failure (measure of asset reliability)

MTTR—Mean Time To Repair (measure of maintainability)

NPV (Net Present Value)—a financial indicator derived from a business case evaluation used to determine the attractiveness of a project. NPV considers the time value of money and calculates (based on an assumed interest rate) what the overall cost and investment dollars would be in each year of the project

Optimized Work (or Optimized Maintenance)—optimal mix of proactive and reactive work and the optimal mix of predictive maintenance based on reliability centered maintenance evaluations

PBP (Pay Back Period)—this is another indicator of project economic feasibility and is the year that cumulative expenditure is equal to the cumulative savings, any time after this point you can expect some return on the investment

P&ID—Process and Instrumentation Drawings

PM (Preventive Maintenance)—work or maintenance tasks based on a set frequency or statistic aimed at arresting or eliminating deterioration of an asset or rebuilding back to its original condition e.g. lubrication and overhauls

PIR (Post Implementation Review)—this is the last phase of the software implementation process and allows for a complete review of the software in use by end users and sets the stage for modifications or changes (of organization, practices and technology components) in order to maximize the benefits from the investment

Proactive Work (or Proactive Maintenance)—maintenance or work done in advance of asset failure, proactive work is always planned

Reactive Work (or Reactive Maintenance)—maintenance or work done after asset failure. Emergency type work is the only type of reactive work that is not planned. All other reactive work should be planned.

Reliability—an indication of the average time an asset can operate with out failing (Mean Time Before Failure is the most common measure of reliability)

Reliability Centered Maintenance—a scientific step-by-step approach to developing maintenance plans for an asset by determining all the various functions, failure modes, consequences combinations and determining the best approach to taking care of the asset

RFI—Request For Information (purchasing tool used to explore the options available in the market place)

RFP—Request For Proposal (purchasing tool used to seek proposal responses from qualified candidates in the market place)

ROI (Rate Of Return)—this is another indicator of project economic feasibility and is the interest rate that makes the overall NPV equal to zero

ROP (Re-Order Point)—this is the minimum stock item balance on hand at which reordering of the item (automatically in the CWMS or manually) is necessary in order to maintain acceptable stores service level for the item.

ROQ (Re Order Quantity)—minimum order quantity purchased when the item reaches the reorder point

SCADA (Supervisory Control And Data Acquisition)—business software the enables automation of assets or groups of assets in a plant, operators can remotely operate and manage these assets by sending commands from a computer screen

SDLC (System Development Life Cycle)—a proven method to proactively manage an integrated technology solution in a world of continuously changing technology

SLA (Service Level Agreements)—internal contracts between organizational groups that sets standards of performance

SOP (Standard Operating Procedure)—standard procedures for operating or maintaining an asset

Three Way Matching—this is a critical step in the invoicing process and refers to the matching of the invoice quantity and item price, to the purchase order item quantity and item price with the item receipt quantity, any exceptions from this process must be corrected before the invoice can be approved

"To Be" work processes—documentation of the new way of working by applying best in class concepts to your existing to eliminate non-value added and redundant activities

TPO (Total Productive Operations), also referred to as TPM (Total Productive Maintenance)—operators trained and certified competent in doing Cleaning, Lubricating, Adjustment, Inspection and Repair (CLAIR) type work allowing the maintenance trades top focus on more core and complex maintenance tasks

WAN (Wide Area Network)—network of LANs through interconnecting cable (fiber optics) or through wireless communications

Work Management Process—refers to the seven step work process common to any work situation - initiation, planning, scheduling, execution, closeout, history and evaluation

Index